Greg Wasinski

Where Faith
&
Real Life
Come Together...

*A discovery in finding hope, God and
who we are in every day interactions.*

By Greg Wasinski

Where Faith & Real Life Come Together...

Cover Design by Frank J. Wasinski III

Printed in the United States of America

ISBN: 978-0-9860269-0-4

Learn more at:
www.GregWasinski.com

Greg Wasinski

Where Faith & Real Life Come Together...

Greg Wasinski

This book is dedicated to my mother Mary Ann. Thank you, Mom, for the gift of faith and every way you offer kindness to others as a child of God.

Where Faith & Real Life Come Together...

What People are Saying...

"Greg Wasinski turned his back on a successful business career to spread the message of the Lord. Greg doesn't just talk the talk, he walks the walk. His book is moving and inspiring."
~ Joe Eszterhas, Author of Crossbearer and Hollywood Screenwriter

"Where Faith & Real Life Come Together is practical and accessible. I wish there were one hundred more books like this that I could recommend to people. Read it. Share it. Live it."
~ Matthew Kelly, author of Rediscovering Catholicism & founder of DynamicCatholic.com

"Greg reminds us that God is found in the stuff of our lives. His stories and insights peel away the layers of our everyday experiences and uncover the faith nuggets embedded there. Easy to read – over and over again."
~ Dr. Bob McCarty, D.Min. Executive Director, National Federation for Catholic Youth Ministry

"Read it. It's simple enough to where it doesn't hurt your brain, but complex enough to where it made me think about my faith life. It was the most helpful faith related book that I have read."
~ Rachel Bailey, High School Teenager

"Many of the reflections are so personal that it seems your sitting next to Greg having a conversation with a friend. And that is the enriching aspect, hearing Greg talk about challenges, victories and moments of awareness that any person can relate to. ...I pray others will enjoy this rich and rewarding book!"
~ Guy Leygraaf, Amazon.com Reviewer

Contents

Where Faith & Real Life Come Together…

Acknowledgements

There are many great and special people who, in one way or another, have touched my life to make this book possible. The long days and long nights it took to write, are nothing in comparison to those who are part of me and have fought by my side to make the dream a reality. There are some people I may miss, but if you truly know me I am hopeful I will have already expressed my gratitude in some way.

My family has always played a tremendous role to shape me into the servant I long to be. Dad, thank you for always providing in the best ways you know how to make sure we could do our best to succeed. Mom, you are beautiful in every way and love at all costs. I am grateful for my brother Frank, from his awesome cover design of this book, to his desire to try and take care of all those around him. The loyalty my brother Rob exudes with passion is unmatched and I know I can always count on him. My sister Jenny is an amazing woman who shows me life should be a little less serious than we make it, and her joy makes my life a brighter place. We are not perfect by any means, but we fight continuously to make all our ancestors proud through whom we strive to be.

For my other "Dad", my father-in-law Roger Boltz. You and Yvonne both met me when I wanted to rule the world. Through the years, you taught me how to let the Lord rule my heart instead. So many things on this journey I owe to you and I have never known someone who can be thousands of miles apart from me, but be standing right next to me when it counts.

I want to thank those who use their religious vocational calling to remind me the power of God's love. Fr. Dan Schlegel, your leadership and guidance led me to where I am and your friendship means so much. Dr. Steve Yates, it was your invitation that opened my eyes to allow God in places I had closed Him out; the living example both you and Adrienne offer is truly Christ's love. Vince Belsito, I do not know a more Spirit filled human being and you have called me to strive into a deeper holiness with your friendship and guidance. Fr. Anthony Zepp, may you rest in peace with God, but know every casual conversation you walked me through changed me forever in some way or another. Fr. Bob Stec, thank you for allowing me to be part of the great ministry work you do. Sister Susan Javorek, you have shown me how compassion and kindness in service is a model to be followed by all.

I am grateful for the friendship of some extraordinary brothers in Christ who lift me up in ways they will never know. Mike Hasychak, you are a great confidant and friend who I am beyond grateful for. Your influence in every breakfast chat had a lot to do with this book being published. Jim Wojtila, I am thankful for the ways you support me through your positive attitude. Eric Leonetti, you have shown me the power of our faith, and your courage to do what is right, really is a great testament to being a man in today's world. Mark Angelotti, you lead by example in your own quiet ways, while lifting me up with your wit and humor. Mike Patin, I never thought you would mentor this "speaker boy" from Cleveland, but you never disappoint me with your friendship, encouragement and efforts to build His kingdom. Thank you Steve Angrisano for the lunch that changed my life to say "yes" and accept I was meant for something bigger. Jesse Manibusan, your generosity, caring and realness are the perfect display of *Where Faith and Real Life Come Together.*

Thank you, Mary Ryan for lending your editing talents to help pull the final product together. You offered your gifts when I needed them most to bring this message full circle.

For those who contributed directly to help push this publication over the top. Your belief in this project, gift of time and treasure humbles me. I will never be able to thank you enough: Mark & Donna Angelotti, Christie & Terry Dilisio, Guy & Nancy Leygraaf, Bill & Mindy Wills, Jackie Vigneault, Irene Hoag, Margaret Vogel, Melissa Olenik, David & Heather Hesse, Mary Ann Bodanza, Karen & Dale Arvay, Bill & Sandy Weil, Denise & Doug Geisler, James & Christine Wale, Theresa & Bill Moision, Patti Tyburski, Jason Cook, Gia Kauffman and in remembrance of Jacqueline Gavorski and Bill Beaver.

My call into ministry might have been ignored or prolonged if it hadn't been for the living example of faith from my very special ministry coordinator, Elizabeth Peterson. You have gifts that are countless and your inspiration always motivates me to work that much harder. We are making the world a better place. So many times when the road is rough and the devil tries to sneak in, you help me see the bright side to believe. Your dedication and complete, unending support is always a blessing… Thanks just thanks.

I am beyond blessed for the love of the greatest gifts I have ever received on this Earth, my children, Nathan and Natalie. You are always patient, when serving God means one less movie night together or one more meal without me; you know we work to help others in all we do. Our family is precious and gives me more strength to keep going than you can realize. I love you both so much and so proud of who you are!

Last but certainly never least, I would still be just a "frog" and not be half the man I am today without my bride, Princess Aimee. I simply love you; you have always been there for me in more ways than I can count and truly been by my side through it all. You brought me to a place to appreciate our faith on a different level and held my hand to take me where you knew I needed to be. I know there are many ups, downs, bumps, bruises and scars we have picked up on our path, but in the end, love wins. To describe how much it all means to me would require words far beyond "thank you." You are an angel.

Where Faith & Real Life Come Together...

Forward

Throughout the Gospels, Jesus used the images and life experiences of ordinary people to communicate the kingdom of God. Bridegrooms and brides, seeds and shrubs, lost coins and treasures, yeast and leaven, lost sheep and banquets all helped point to the mystery of God. Furthermore, it helped Jesus' followers know that he understood their culture and world. He was not a God of faraway places but a God who walked with them, understood their world and helped them to see the presence of the Divine made real in their midst.

The fact remains that ordinary life teaches us a great deal about the kingdom of God even today. Each new day, each person and each experience is, potentially, a sacramental encounter teaching us about and pointing to the presence of God. In joy and celebration, in sorrow and loss, in challenge and affirmation, God speaks to us where we are and is made real in our midst. However, in a world filled with distractions, busyness and abundance, it is a greater challenge than ever to discover the extraordinary presence of God in the ordinary experiences of our lives.

"Where Faith & Real Life Come Together..." points to those every day experiences which convey the wisdom, grace and the compassion of God. Through personal storytelling, Scriptural references and astute observation, author Greg Wasinski takes the "stuff" of his life and shows us how it reveals God's presence near. In family and friendship, through experience and familiar images, Greg draws wisdom and understanding as to how God communicates to us in the ordinary, everyday events of our lives. Each chapter lets us explore the sacramental encounters of our own lives and what we learn about ourselves, about others and about our God.

Each chapter of the book offers wisdom to savor and questions for our own reflection, consideration and prayer. May these pages provide a window through which we look at our lives in a new way and encounter God's extraordinary presence in the ordinariness of our lives.

Fr. Dan Schlegel, Pastor
Church of the Holy Angels
Chagrin Falls, Ohio

Greg Wasinski

Preface

This book is set up to allow you to have time to read and then reflect how each chapter directly relates to your personal situation. The writings are kept on the shorter side in an effort to capture your attention. They are not meant to "beat you over the head" with a personal view, but to allow you to apply it where needed in your life.

The manner in which you would like to reflect on the book in its entirety is your choice. You can read it all the way through at your leisure, use the thirty-one chapters as a devotional for a month or you may simply look at the titles and find the ones which immediately seem to relate to your needs. It really is written in a style to help you encounter faith in a way that is best for YOU.

Why the Bee?

TM

At the beginning of each chapter, you will notice a "bee" symbol. This bee, as illustrated, is the logo for "Let Me Be..." Ministries (my speaking ministry). It is a simple reminder that each of us is called to *be nothing more than God created us to be.* You may see this bee displayed proudly wherever you hear me give a talk or wherever people have received a take home item from one of my ministry events. It's my hope the bee will give you a little peace of mind, knowing that as we go through our present days, despite life's pressures, it's okay simply to slow down and *"just be..."*

Introduction

Before we start, I want you to know wherever you are in your life or faith journey, it's okay. Whatever religious denomination you are, it's okay. Whether you feel you are broken to a point that's not repairable or riding high and thankful for everything you have, it's okay. Whether you bought this book for a good read or are hoping to develop a deeper faith formation, it's okay. If you are not sure why someone gave you this book, it's okay. Or if you are just trying to figure out what God might have in store for your life, it's okay. I am just like you, and throughout my entire life I have experienced *every* one of the thoughts mentioned above during some period. I can honestly say, until I accepted this idea of whatever happened or wherever I was, "It's okay," I really couldn't understand just how blessed and how fortunate I was to be loved in such an unending manner. This book is a journey,not a chronicle, a guide, not a manual, a reflection,not a Gospel. I believe what I write is meant to be shared to allow others to know we are not alone, no matter what.

Allow me to share a little information about myself. I am a convert into ministry after spending 15 years as a corporate executive. I do not have a theology degree, nor am I a religious scholar. I am just a man who finally realized his blessings and responsibility to go deeper into faith to bring about hope through the word of God. I work harder, read more scripture and study deeper now to be educated. The original path I took in life was not a plan to enter into a vocation of service to the Lord. I grew up in a family with strong Catholic roots which carried over from my ancestors' immigration from Poland. I believe it was this type of foundation that eventually brought my wife into our faith the year of our marriage. I have not always been a model Christian and I am sad to say that I even spent a brief period of time away from the church. I am grateful God never stopped searching for me to bring me back. I heard my call to transfer my talents and work in the church because, when I looked back at my life, I could see all the places God was already using me and the amazing difference it would make when I accepted His path for me. He placed people in my life who were willing to show me where I belong and how I could make a difference in my community. I assure you, there are many ups and downs with the life my family has chosen to live as we work to inspire others to be difference makers in the world. One thing is for certain though, we have been protected and provided for all along the way by a God who never breaks a promise. Finding faith in real life is the only way I believe we can fully accept life for the blessing it is, regardless of our circumstances or the people we encounter along the way.

In preparing for a national conference, I was asked by the person creating my ad for the program, "If you had to sum up in one line what your message is for the youth and adults you speak to, what would it be?" The answer came very quickly to me, "Where faith and real life come together." This is the struggle I believe so many children of God deal with continuously. We think there will be lightning bolts, locusts and the brightest shining stars when God is truly at work in our lives. The fact of the matter is, usually it's a stranger who opens a door, the child who holds our hand or a friend who calls us out of the blue. It becomes our job to see that although faith is grounded in the core of our belief, it only becomes "real" when we go out and live it. Within the perfectly-imperfect church, there is a realization that sometimes people can disappoint us and only *we* can truly control how we become the hands and feet of Christ out in the world. It's up to us to help build communities that prosper through example and offer a willingness to find God where He is coming to us.

During a presentation for incoming freshman at a high school, I was telling my personal conversion story about how the Lord spoke directly to me while on retreat. One of the students I made eye contact with just blurted out in wide eyed amazement, "He spoke to you!?!?" After a chuckle, I said, "Yes, and before I experienced it, I can pretty much say I would have reacted as you just did and possibly thought the speaker in front of me might be insane." I went on to explain how His voice is not the thunderous rumbling and bellowing portrayed in some interpretations of the story of creation in the book of Genesis. No, it is a gentle whisper, a compassionate conversation, or for me, just a disappointing or stern, "*Greg!*" The reason we discount His voice is because it's not what we want. Additionally, what usually happens is we tune God out because in our minds it cannot be real. We feel it doesn't make logical sense we would be "hearing" the words not through our ears but within the deepest part of our being. When He is trying to get our attention, just know it is heard in our hearts because that is where love lives, where He dwells and where He can always find us.

The beauty of where faith and real life actually come together is that God does meet us where we are. Life happens and many things shape us into the people we are. There doesn't have to be some tragedy, or some great loss, for our faith to be shaped or even for us to become different people. Quite frankly, we need to appreciate the times we can find God without having to run to Him for healing. This book will hopefully help you to see all the interactions that occur daily where God is at work. He is preparing us for great things and holding us when bad things happen. Take time to place your life in His hands and find ways you can connect to the stories written and the ways people are affected in the world around us. Yes, His love is enough on so many days, and it just has to be, in a world where hopes can be often overshadowed by reality; you have the power to change that. Life is about what we relate to and not always the misfortune someone else has had happen to them. Breathe it in, take it in and allow yourself to recognize hope is about much more than personal prayer, it's about everyday living!

Even in the midst of writing this book, I am reminded over and over again it is necessary for faith and real life to come together. I long for extended periods of isolation, the quiet times specifically designated for writing. Yet life does not stop and my family still has demands. So, I continue on and write in small openings of free time or sneak off to get in a voice recording so the next thought doesn't escape me. There is no perfect time that makes it easy to just sit and tap away on the keys of my laptop, but since this book is about where faith and real life come together, I guess it's very fitting the manner it's authored falls along the same lines. Sure, sometimes a bit of guilt can creep in when I'm taking time away while the family is off enjoying a moment together watching a movie. But I know in my heart, by doing things to make a better world, God will never take away time He won't give back in the end. In it all, the challenge even to write reminds me our prayers and faithfulness must fit into the reality of our lives because that is how they are answered. We live in a real world with real human needs which God uses to walk with us, providing what is best. When we want to be one with Him, sometimes we are able to get quiet moments, but in the fast pace of life, the only way to true happiness and fulfillment is to find Him in everyday occurrences and living.

I love one of the final scenes in the climax of the movie *Joshua* which has the human version of Christ sitting at the feet of the Pope in the Vatican. When the Pope realizes it is truly Jesus with him, he asks His Lord, "What do you want me to tell them (his people)?" With tender eyes, Joshua looks at him and softly says, "Simply tell them that the story hasn't changed and the message is still the same. Just tell them that I love them." As you read on in this book, the message is still the same; He loves us. If we live out our lives of faith in that same manner of love and respect, what a better place we will have to walk with each other. Hopefully, we will realize no matter what high or low we face, God is present and no matter what He is there to give nothing but love.

NOTE: Every chapter of this book begins with a title and then two quotes. The first quote is a scripture verse that directly relates to the overall subject of "FAITH" highlighted in the chapter. If you already study scripture, use this as the basis to go deeper into your understanding of how it relates to you. If this is all new, allow each particular Bible verse be a start to deepen your own spiritual journey. The second quote in each chapter is an inspirational, "REAL LIFE" quote from various people in the world who have offered a positive message in line with the theme of what is about to be read. When we can connect the dots in this manner with all facets of life, we will find where faith and real life become one.

In closing, take one deep breath in of *faith* and exhale one long whisper of *reality*. Close your eyes for thirty seconds and offer a prayer for your heart to be opened and all your reservations to be released. Be open, be God's, and most importantly, just be...

Chapter 1

Why You Watch the Game...

__FAITH:__ *"I urge you, brothers, in the name of our Lord Jesus Christ, that all of you agree in what you say, and that there be no divisions among you, but that you be united in the same mind and in the same purpose."* ~1Corinthians 1:10

__REAL LIFE:__ *"When you turn to God, you discover He has been facing you all the time."* ~Zig Ziglar

I once had a conversation with some people who were discussing why they don't attend a worship service or mass regularly. It was interesting because none of them seemed to be angry with organized religion, and from what I surmised they weren't distant for any reason other than plain old apathy. In

their eyes (and in their words, not mine), they had no particular need to praise God in a place of worship; nothing awful was happening at that particular moment requiring a need for extra support. A busy lifestyle with career, kids' events and other obligations left them working hard to have the life they were entitled to have, so why go? I had to think about this for a moment because for a period in my life, I was the person who was offering the same type of misguided rationale of why I didn't need to go to church.

I asked them this simple question, "Do you watch sports?" They replied, "Yes." I followed that up with, "Okay, well do you root for a particular team and if so, why would you do that?" Without allowing them to answer verbally, because their heads were already nodding, I began to offer them a correlation between faith communities and various forms of sporting entertainment which defines some of the things driving us to watch the game. We really don't need to watch the game to be a sports fan, nor is it the only way to find out whether our team is the best or not. We can simply tell who is best by the outcome of the final score and see the stats at the conclusion of the match. So realistically, we have to conclude, that isn't the whole story of why you watch the game.

Part of the reason we watch the game is to

be entertained. When we physically go to games to cheer on our team in person, we want to feel we've given them a little boost to push them to victory. Likewise, we might watch the game on TV with a bunch of other fans so we can be part of a group, otherwise known as a community. Within this small community of fellow fans, we are able to share our joys when our team comes out on top and sorrow, or even tears, when there is a loss during a time when we felt so optimistic. (I'm from Cleveland, so let's not go there). Upon laying out the reasons why we gather to be part of sporting events, I followed it all up with, "It sounds a lot like church to me."

Bringing it full circle, when supporting our fellow men and women, faith is no different than why you watch the game. We don't have to worship or go to a church building for mass to say we believe. Life still goes on and we just know God is there and will clean up our messes as needed. It's our understanding He won't do bad things to us because we were taught somewhere along the way He is ever loving and forgives the unforgivable. But just like why you watch the game, allow me to explain why you need to attend church.

Just as a young athlete will watch a player to learn techniques and see first-hand how to be the best, we go to church to learn and be inspired. All of God's work and His stories are being laid out in front of us so we can understand why we have to go through trials or setbacks. He shows us how we should appreciate the good times of each and every victory that is granted. When we are part of a faith community, we share an unbreakable bond only this type of unity can offer and only a "me" type of mentality can destroy. We must journey together for so many reasons but especially for the times when the outcome is not as we imagined it, but as God wants it. In the game, we are entertained. It takes our minds off reality. In worship, we are reassured that reality has an ultimate purpose and we are never left alone. Those people in the seats next to us, and those who attend faith based community events, are there to be our own personal fan base. They cheer us on with what we believe when we have nothing left to give ourselves. Matthew 18:20 reminds us, *"For where two or three are gathered together in my name, there am I in the midst of them."* It's made so easy for us; all we need to do is seek out others and offer support.

So I will tell you "why you watch the game." It's because you are hopeful and you believe your team can always win no matter what. God calls you to be on His team; with Him each week because He believes in you the very same way. His promise says, *"At the end of the day I will never let you lose.*" However, it isn't always enough just to be a good person. Remember, the reason you might attend isn't always because of what you need at that moment, but what others around you might need from your simple presence and living example.

Why do you "watch the game" of sports, life and faith?

What is a role that is so important for you to play in your own community?

Today I will…

Chapter 2

Prayer, It's a Simple Conversation...

<u>FAITH:</u> *"Rejoice always. Pray without ceasing. In all circumstances give thanks, for this is the will of God for you in Christ Jesus." ~1Thessalonians 5:16-18*

<u>REAL LIFE:</u> *"The value of consistent prayer is not that He will hear us, but that we will hear Him." ~William McGill*

Many people struggle when it comes to finding time to pray or even be secure enough that their prayer is being offered in the "correct manner." Yes, our days are filled with countless tasks and activities, but they actually become perfect times to simply talk with God. After all, He just wants us to remember Him at all times and to take moments within the hectic portions of life to have a simple conversation with Him.

Prayer reminds me a lot of the front porch chats we get to have with ancestors who can offer more wisdom in a twenty minute conversation than we might get from a whole year in school. You know, those times we look back on and cherish, saying, "Why didn't I listen more intently and savor those brilliant words?" Our talks with God are no different. He can help provide a peace and understanding within us much faster through prayer than any of the other temporary distractions from our problems we attempt to use. It all starts by us taking the time to have a simple conversation.

Looking at it in a different manner, at a young age we are taught prayers to recite like, "Now I lay me down to sleep..." or "Bless us, O Lord, and these Thy gifts..." to help us grow in faith and place our trust in God. Additionally, we follow a patterned model of those we look up to and how they might offer up a rosary or pray scripture on their knees at their bedside. No matter how we have learned to pray, at some point our faith outgrows all particular models of prayer and we need to begin to have simple conversations with God. It's no different than how we have learned things as children and over time work to master them as adults. When we grow up we become better and more comfortable at many things; prayer is one of them, if we allow it.

It is absolutely necessary for prayer to become a simple conversation. Our lives change, our needs change and our emotional desire to connect with God changes. If we already have a deep relationship with God, then it needs to move to a new level where we are listening more for what He desires from us than we are asking from Him. For those who are beginning a deeper discovery of faith, it's comforting to know that when it comes to prayer, we are all in the same place. We do not always have to commit a bunch of words to memory, but rather, just open our hearts and our minds to simply talk with God. Ultimately, once our hearts are open, we will have gotten quiet enough to hear the answers to some of the things we ask. Once our words are offered up, we need to fill ourselves with a silence that allows His answer to be poured back into us. Hearing His words fully, is the most comforting way to enter into a deeper relationship with Him. This example was given to us long ago by Moses as he led the Israelites out of Egypt. He was deeply devoted to God's plan, but often abandoned traditional prayer to find a secluded spot on a mountain to question and converse with God.

Sometimes our prayer life even works out like phone calls we place to people we really don't want to talk to. We pray to get voice mail so we do not have to have a conversation, but just rather lay out what we want. So when God actually answers our prayers we are stunned and shocked. The conversation does not always go in the direction we planned. I firmly believe there are people in this world who walk away from their beliefs because they have substantial prayer growth and it scares them; they feel broken or less faithful because their routine changes. It can become commonplace for a person who has memorized specific prayers to just recite them without thinking. They reach a level of comfort, which develops over time into boredom, causing the reverence to slip and their mind to wander. This change is not a sign they are broken, it is a call to a deeper relationship where they can be fulfilled in unimaginable ways.

When we think about our prayer, we cannot have a better model than what Jesus gave us. In addition to providing us with what we now know as the "Our Father" or the "Lord's Prayer," we witness examples in the Bible of *how* He prayed as a human. In my mind, I have this vision of Jesus praying in the Garden on the night He was to be seized and handed over for crucifixion. In His sadness and His fear, His prayers were not lifted up as final demands or detailed ways

His Father could change the course of His purpose; He prayed for reassurance. *"He advanced a little and fell prostrate in prayer, saying, 'My Father, if it is possible, let this cup pass from me; yet, not as I will, but as you will'"* (Matthew 26:39). This conversation with God not only shows us that Jesus prayed for what He feared, but also prayed with an acceptance to be open to the answer.

With so many daily events where we do not have control, we need to be open and listen to what God is saying to us. It really is funny how we think we have our own plans and then God lets us know He is in charge. The gift of prayer is a direct access to God which provides us with the one-on-one time we long for. I understand prayer doesn't always change the outcome of what happens, but does grant us an acceptance of our situation and quite possibly recognition of our duties. For these reasons, prayer is the answer for all of our emotions. Pray when you are angry, happy, sad, confused, and thankful or just want to offer a petition for someone else.

Finally, ask yourself the question, "If God's prayer inbox had different folders, how would mine be sorted?" Do we take the time to converse with God in thanksgiving, as well as requests? Don't forget that our own healing through prayer can be attained by how much we are praying for others, because we are then reminded of how truly blessed we are. God wants different things than we want and it's okay if we don't always get our way. Most times, prayer just needs to be a simple conversation, reminding us that, the only wrong way to pray is NOT to pray.

Name some recent times in your life when you were not listening or fully engaged in prayer.

What are some ways you can deepen your prayer life and reconnect with God?

Today I will...

Chapter 3

God's Time...

FAITH: *"For the vision is a witness for the appointed time, a testimony to the end; it will not disappoint. If it delays, wait for it, it will surely come, it will not be late."* ~ Habakkuk 2:3

REAL LIFE: *"There are two kinds of people: those who say to God, 'Thy will be done,' and those to whom God says, 'All right, then, have it your way.'"* ~C.S. Lewis

Imagine for a moment if CNN had been around in the time of Jesus. Even better yet, at the point of creation or even during the days in which the prophets worked to give us what we now know in the Hebrew Scriptures. The news would have traveled way too fast, and criticism too furious! How quickly word of their mission would have been reported in a distorted manner by minds too shallow to digest the significance of it all. News anchors would have added their own agendas and their own spins to create a sensationalized story built to destroy the beauty of God's purpose and create division for the masses. This type of scenario seems to happen almost every day now. Our children (as well as us) have become part of a society which needs information instantaneously. Many times incorrect information or views are offered up in an effort to be the first to get it in our hands. We are no longer able to wait to receive the full story and form our own beliefs because everything is spoon fed to us with a twist. The reality we get depends on which of the papers we read, web sites we visit or any one of the 350 television channels we may have watched.

For the prophets, authors of the Bible, and Jesus, things happened in the manner in which God intended and on *His time*. The living word grew from the center out with deep-rootedness. A concentrated message that spread through those who were able to give a first-hand witness of all accounts. It was absolutely necessary for the foundation of our faith to stem from passion and commitment, rather than the spontaneous need for empty inspiration sought by so many in a time of need. God needs to make sure we are ready for the grace He bestows upon us and we can fully process what we are experiencing. We are humans who are striving to get to a place we know is better than this Earth; it's not supposed to be our time, it's Kairos, meaning "God's Time."

Let me give you this scenario: As parents, we continually tell our children they will get exactly what they are asking for after their chores are done. This type of implied vision is completely incomprehensible to our darling youngsters, so the bottom immediately falls out from this level of thinking. What often follows are hours of arguing, stomping and yelling. This behavior prevents them from receiving what they ultimately would have gotten if they just would have done their task and accepted the road to their reward. As they try to tactfully explain their reasoning, then plead and finally start to whine, they grow further and further away from what they were fighting for in the first place. In the same manner, we argue with God because we want things right now! We lose our own focus and dwell on what we didn't get, rather than what we do have. It's important to take a step back to realize He is not always saying, *"No"* to our requests, but more like, *"Do what I ask first because I know what is best for you."*

In life they say, "timing is everything" and it's true in faith. Just as we watch over and parent, God parents us. God knows what is best and what the best time for everything is. The prayers you offer today are not the same as they will be three months from now. Additionally, the way you see or understand the answers to those prayers will also be very different. So maybe each prayer you are about to offer up should start with a quick prayer for the patience to be worthy of the answer. It's not the decisions that prepare us for what is going to happen, it's how everything happens that prepares us for what we receive.

Looking back, I now recognize that God had the best intention of timing when…

What are the areas it is most important that I pray for patience regarding immediate future decisions?

Today I will…

Chapter 4

Whatever it Takes...

FAITH: *"By faith Noah, warned about what was not yet seen, with reverence built an ark for the salvation of his household. Through this he condemned the world and inherited the righteousness that comes through faith."*
~*Hebrews 11:7*

REAL LIFE: *"Do not pray for easy lives. Pray to be stronger men."* ~*John F. Kennedy*

Traveling around to various rallies and faith based conventions gives me a chance to see so many great people offering quality ministry. The ministry professionals who are so good at what they do are completely open to whatever message the Holy Spirit is calling them to deliver. The themes widely vary, so the overall message can be completely different even if the scripture or music is the same. In preparation for a youth convention, a friend of mine, Jennifer Kilo, asked me for some thoughts regarding her diocese' youth convention, "Whatever It Takes." My immediate reaction was to say, "I have no idea what that means." However, as I pondered deeper into it, I thought of how great a message it really is for all of us.

I love how the message of "whatever it takes" is all encompassing wherever we need to apply it. It is the defining statement which shows people you might do a little something if you kind of believe, but when you have conviction, you go all out. A strong statement such as this is the same kind of call when Paul said, *"Let no one have contempt for your youth, but set an example for those who believe, in speech, conduct, love, faith, and purity"* (1Timothy 4:12). "Youth" is a relational term in how we choose to reflect on this line for our own lives. Yes, we have the literal definition which lets our young people know they always have a voice and are responsible for their actions. However, the word "youth" can describe how qualified each of us feels to evangelize or share our faith. There are times we may think because we are not called into a vocation of religious life, we may be unworthy or viewed negatively by others with various theologically related credentials. Fact is, we are always learning in life and should view our faith through child-like eyes to allow openness for us to be sent forth and display our faith in a manner helping others to believe. Regardless of age or experience, do whatever it takes.

Along the same lines, all the authors used specific words in the Bible to create feelings with very explicit descriptions about what it takes to be faithful. Jesus didn't just die, He suffered. People didn't just pray, they fell to their knees. God just doesn't like us, He loves us unconditionally. We are not called simply to just try, we are asked to surrender. Even Noah found it absolutely necessary to place all his trust in the Lord and, at all costs, work tirelessly to build the ark as he was commanded despite the doubters all around him. I could go on and on, but I invite you to think of your own words which help you relate to the manner in which God is really speaking to you.

For me, the phrase "whatever it takes" really is about so much more. I want to take all of this one step further and identify each of the words in this phrase individually. When a prayer is powerful or words in the Bible speak to us, we need to pick them apart one by one and let their application be all encompassing in our lives.

WHATEVER – The strong and open word saying you will think outside the box to be different really means *however, anything* or *no matter what.* You will be creative, you will show passion, and take the opportunity to use original thinking. By doing this, you will set everything in motion and get more people to notice your faith in a way they may not have before. Be open and flexible to roll with the punches.

IT - The main *identifier*, the *noun*, the *point*, the *idea*...what are you going to do? What is the one thing which shows people you have something special to share? How will you react to a particular situation when it may not be the easiest decision to make? This is the piece of the puzzle that ultimately will reveal where your beliefs are. "It" is not just the basis of our faith, but also the choices we make; this is what you will take into the world to be Christ's example. Others will use "it" as a starting point for their own journey.

TAKES - The *fulfillment*, the *verb*, the *doing*, the *proof*. You've identified how and what you feel needs to be done, but this aspect of "takes" completes your character. What do we do to take our thoughts of how we want to go out and be the living model, turning them into living proof through action? It means nothing if it just remains a nice little notion in our head. This will be the manner in which your testimony overcomes real world thinking and you go out to do something about it.

Doing whatever it takes, means it's one thing to be involved, but quite another to be committed. It needs to be an "all in" level of thinking where you do everything to fight for what you believe. It's up to you to fulfill your conviction through positive methods of example out in the world. It's important that we continually remind ourselves how ultimately faith is never fully explained in words but rather it is understood through actions.

You have heard my thoughts, and now it is time for your conviction to take over. Pray on these words and fill in the blanks as to what their meanings are to you.

WHATEVER -

IT -

TAKES -

Today I will...

Chapter 5

Chloe ~ A Loss of Unconditional Love...

FAITH: *"For out of much affliction and anguish of heart I wrote to you with many tears, not that you might be pained but that you might know the abundant love I have for you."* ~2Corinthians 2:4

REAL LIFE: *"The pain passes, but the beauty remains."* ~*Pierre Auguste Renoir*

    As someone who longs to always bring about inspiration in my message, it's not often I want to write from one of the darkest places in my life. That said, it is sometimes necessary for us to put our thoughts down on paper or pour out our hearts in times of crisis, a form of proof in whether we actually believe what we say. In January of 2012, I was reminded once again how life teaches repeat lessons to never take anything for granted. The following are my words as listed in my journal entry, intended to be a reflection giving you a perspective of it from my eyes. I have decided to keep the integrity of my feelings intact from the day we had to say good bye to a faithful companion, rather than reword them specifically for publication. The day was a bitter pill of how truly special the little things in life are. Each of us will have our own application, time and time again, for special people, pets and relationships we lose during life's journey. Make the following your own and draw a relation to your own life in whatever manner you might need to.

Monday morning, on my wife Aimee's birthday, our German Shepherd, Chloe, suffered a stroke at 6:00 a.m. that forced us to take a frantic trip to an emergency veterinary hospital where we eventually had to say goodbye to "our baby before we had babies." We went as a family and made "team" choices for what the future of our dear companion should be; I wanted us to be "one" to signify how special she was as a member of the Wasinski clan. We just didn't lose a friend that day, no it was much deeper, losing Chloe was a loss of "unconditional love."

Chloe was a simple pound puppy (with ears 3 times too big for her head) that we got at 6 weeks old in 1996 when I had lots of hair and kids were not in our future for another 3 ½ years. She was the dog neither of us ever had growing up and we knew she was perfect because she was born on my birthday (I say this with a smile). But really what she grew into over her 15 year life span was a "protector" of our children , before and after they were born, a "cuddle partner" when I went through 3 different surgeries and most of all she was the giver of "unconditional love" at all times; something that is impossible to get from any human. We expected we were getting one thing when we adopted her, and through all the years I reflect on, she gave us so much more than I could have ever dreamed of. Chloe was a sense of security despite a hectic home and part of us in every way.

I look at the gift Chloe was to us, and in all of my sorrow, I need to see her as another creation of the love God sends to us on this Earth. Much like Chloe, our God is always there for us despite our original expectations of what He is supposed to be in our own mind. Even though we leave him in the background some days, He longs to greet us only with love and comfort for our rough moments, regardless of who anyone else thinks we are or the failures that might have occurred in our lives. I can even draw the parallel that our relationship with pets is a clear correlation to the same manner in which we are called to be caretakers for humanity; for those that rely on us to feed them, to nurture them and to take care of their needs when they cannot do it for themselves. We long for physical affection and we are given it in so many wonders of creation but even for me, it now has to be about both the "seen and unseen" reminders of the gift Chloe was; she changed our lives forever. I long to turn any corner of my house and see her panting and waiting for me to just give her one little pet or any sign of love.

The kids wanted to be with Chloe when she passed and as much as I struggled with them being witnesses to her last breaths, there was a lesson in it all that they were meant to be part of. My daughter Natalie said on the way home, "Dad at least we are not like Mary and Joseph", to which I asked, "Why do you say that?" And this little 9 year old child reminded me, that despite our tears we were still blessed. Natalie gave us her understanding of sorrow in the moment, "Well Mary and Joseph had to watch their loved one and Son suffer, Chloe is no longer in pain and she just peacefully went to sleep"... After all, isn't it what we all long for when we move into our final rest? To be surrounded by those you love while you enter into a world of no more struggles. This conversation made me realize once again that my children get it because of our faith. The same comfort we once gained by Chloe's physical presence was now being given through the Maker who breathed life into her.

I am not going to get into the religious or theological discussions about whether or not dogs go to Heaven, but I believe MINE did. Not only is she there to be restored to her puppy like exuberance, but I know she is there to be a companion to those who wait to be reunited with their loved ones. One thing that I absolutely know for certain is that Chloe would give a loud bark and a giant tug on an Angel's wings for a divine defender to come to our aid if we ever needed a guardian in a desperate situation... proving to me once again, that she will be our faithful protector today and always.

A flood of emotion rushes back into me as I read these words long after the event. Although painful, it is proof I still believe every word I said that day knowing what a gift from God Chloe was. I know each of us relies on someone or something to prove the real presence of Christ in the world. It's necessary for us to find Him in all the reminders placed on this Earth; so many days we long for a Jesus with "skin on" to help us believe. It's Christ who has taken on flesh and blood form in another person, to be as real as we need Him to be during crisis and heartache.

I still miss our Chloe tremendously and even though we have a new companion, she will always be the dog who was there during some of the most monumental growth periods for our family. We never look to replace her because that would be impossible, but I can assure you, together we are more aware of the lessons she taught us. Chloe's example allows us to find unconditional love in many places out in the world we may not have noticed before.

How do I recognize the beauty of the creatures or people that represent God's love for me?

The story that comes to mind that shows me a true display of unconditional love is…

Today I will…

Chapter 6

For Sale...

FAITH: *"What profit would there be for one to gain the whole world and forfeit his life? Or what can one give in exchange for his life?"* ~Matthew 16:26

REAL LIFE: *"Watch your thoughts; they become words. Watch your words; they become actions. Watch your actions; they become habits. Watch your habits; they become character. Watch your character; it becomes your destiny."* ~Unknown

Real estate values are pretty low these days. More and more people often sell below what they think their home value is worth just because panic has set in. Sadly though, the "fire sale" is not just happening in property; it's happening within our very selves as people. Because the world demands so much from us and advertisers make us think we need to buy more, have more and possess the latest and greatest, we fall into a trap of thinking we are not worth as much as we truly are (or end up forgetting it). So, the result is we sell out, becoming less than who we are called to be. But, we need to ask ourselves, "At what cost are we for sale?"

Day in and day out, we make choices that are not conducive to being the people we want to be. We gossip, act out, fall into old habits, make unhealthy choices or potentially even end up back in the same crowd we wanted to get away from. Falling victim to these temptations is not always an intentional act, but sometimes it can be. We can become trapped into thinking we are no better than our past and fall victim to influences that held us back in the first place. We may sell out because in the moment, it is easier to leave our values aside. Making a decision that has short term, feel good benefits, rather than looking at the long term effects our own regret will play on us. We are pushed and pushed by daily influences to want more, want less, be more, be less and on and on. You have to trust in your faith and believe in yourself enough to hold yourself accountable to be who you want and not allow yourself to be for sale.

If you have placed yourself on that market of

being for sale, or even sold out at one point, it doesn't mean you can't go back and take hold of who you desire to be once more. Fight for it, and know you deserve better. You want to make improvements that make you proud of the life you are living. I like to say, "You must make a dwelling place within you so others want to visit, and when they walk away, they feel as if they are better because of you." I saw another quote once which said, "Today's trial is tomorrow's testimony." It's true, if we don't have instances where we have fallen or received battle scars, then others can't buy in to believing we know how to get up.

Jesus asked His disciples, *"Who do you say that I am?"* (Mark 8:29) Well, today I would like to ask you the question a little differently, with a twist. I believe Jesus was asking: *"Who do you say you are?"* Within His original question to the disciples, I think Jesus was looking to see how much they had learned from His teachings and what they witnessed as His followers. It was critical in their role as disciples for them to believe in Jesus in accordance with the faith Christ was instilling in them; a faith reliant on the type of leaders they would become. It had to go beyond what they were part of with Jesus as a human. He would not always be there to run back to when the non-believers pressed them for answers. They had to be better than everyone else because they had made a choice to be part of something only a few could handle. He was going to entrust His ministry to them, and they had to know His purpose was not only about Him coming to be the Messiah, but to teach them how they would be accountable for the church when He was gone. Most importantly, Christ needed to know they could not be for sale in His absence. Even today, He has entrusted you with the same responsibility with His church. He needs you to know who you say you are, so you can lead by example of the seen and unseen.

You are not for sale and neither is what you believe. When we find ourselves in that moment of NOT being who we want to be, we have to think it all the way through and then plot our course of action. Your attitude, mood, and sheer presence affect the lives of the people around you. You are responsible to more than yourself. If you have already made the decision to try and be better, then remember you are already ahead of the game and you will come out on top.

The biggest challenges I deal with daily that lead me away from who I strive to be are...

What are ways I can work to not "sell out" my values or faith when at school, work or out in the world?

Today I will...

Chapter 7

Starting Over...

FAITH: *"So whoever is in Christ is a new creation: the old things have passed away; behold, new things have come."* ~2Corinthians 5:17

REAL LIFE: *"In any moment of decision the best thing you can do is the right thing, the next best thing is the wrong thing, and the worst thing you can do is nothing."* ~Theodore Roosevelt

I once suffered an injury which caused an extended layoff from consistent exercise. During this period, I learned how important it really is for me to have an exercise routine as part of my weekly schedule. Working out just doesn't physically fuel me, it gives me the mental strength to refresh me and relieve the stresses of my day. I admit though, no matter how committed anyone is, it's always hard to *start over* after they have fallen so far from where they worked exhaustingly hard to be.

Anytime you set out to reach a goal, the journey is filled with many triumphs and its fair share of defeats; my story to get back to being healthy was no different. After working tirelessly for two years to lose fifty pounds, I pushed my body beyond its limits and hurt my right shoulder. So for a few months I struggled through routines which were only *half* of what I was doing before. Then, because of my own frustrations, a few months later the exercise sessions dwindled to *half of a half*. Finally, I surrendered to the mental battle and gave up to be consumed by life. I flat out just stopped working out all together. The end result...I gained twenty-five of those pounds back over a period of nine months.

We all have different reasons why we hesitate to pull up our boot straps and begin again after a hiccup with any endeavor. In my situation, the real reason I had to start over is not really because I hurt myself, it was because I didn't accept that only a single part of me was "broken." I still could have continued to give my best in other areas by working out the rest of my body which wasn't injured. I had to force myself to take a step back and realize it was about me feeling sorry for myself. I was pouting and wasn't exercising unless I could do it the way I *always* do. Since I couldn't do the type of workouts I wanted to, it wasn't as exciting to me and I felt like a failure. The sense that it was a lost cause would trickle down and move into me eating even more because, "Who cares, if I can't work out I might as well enjoy myself in other ways." You don't get very far with that thinking because life doesn't work that way.

It's so troubling when we have to start over because we've allowed ourselves to succumb to old habits destroying all we do to be better people. Most cases of giving up have deeper consequences than just the temporary end result. For my story, the effects were not purely physical; because my mind stopped training it hampered my ability to positively focus on the road to recovery. It was saying, "Forget it, you will not get back to where you want to be," while my heart was saying, "You have to start somewhere and I know you can get back to where you were before." It didn't seem to happen in my time or as fast as I would have liked, but I did make it back to my goal weight through consistency. I looked at it through a lens in which each day had to be a starting over of its own. A process to begin again had to start with changing my attitude of acceptance relative to where I was at this moment.

Our relationship with God can be similar to these theories of exercise when it comes to *starting over*. If we do not call on Him for *spiritual workouts* through conversation and praise, we get out of *spiritual shape*. What begins to happen is we miss His voice when He speaks to us. Consequently, we turn a blind eye to blessings and are not in the condition necessary to help lift others up. Let this moment be a defining one which says, "If you have not had the relationship in faith that you wanted or think you should have, it is okay, come back and start over. If your marriage is struggling or your parenting is strained, it is okay, come back and start over. If you have lost who you want to be or life has overwhelmed you, it's okay, come back and start over." Hope is a limitless boundary and has no memory of the past; it is the single most important tool allowing us to redirect our life towards fulfillment. Focus on starting over.

The gym was always there for me and I could go work out anytime I wanted because it's open twenty-four hours a day. However, because the workout routines weren't going to go according to my plans, I did not go at all. The absence of training meant I did not feed my body with what it craved. In the same manner, we seek a relationship with God and He is always there for us 24/7, accepting us however we come. If we cannot come to him 100% on a particular day, He understands saying, *"Give me your best and I will still fill and provide you with the benefit of my love."* God is looking for consistency of effort, not short bursts of desire. It's not about only sprinting to Him when we are empty to be refilled. It can't work that way because it will never happen fast enough or in the right manner in order to fix us on the spot. Strength in our days can come from the simple exercises of prayer which keep us mentally fit. Prayers that include, "Thank you" when you wake up, a midday offering for another person who needs it more than we do and a, "Thank you" once again at bed time. This repetition centers us to find all the blessings in our life and eliminates the darkness trying to force the good to the wayside. Each day is a chance to start over in God's eyes and begin again on the path He calls us to.

Don't walk away from your beliefs because you can't fulfill expectations your current state of mind prevents you from accomplishing. You have to know, your longing to experience God's grace is not gone, and you might just be blocking the habits which yielded results. When all else fails and we are weak on our own, we must rely on not only the spiritual existence of God, but also where He exists in the world. There are tremendous people willing to support us, who will help us be who we are called to be. It's so important we all believe within ourselves enough to know that whatever good habits we fall away from, we can get back to them anytime we want through belief. Simply walk back to that imaginary line today and begin to journey again by starting over.

What have I gotten away from that has caused me to get out of "shape"?

What affect(s) has this caused on my life? How can I change it?

Today I will…

Chapter 8

I Have You...

FAITH: *"You whom I have taken from the ends of the earth and summoned from its far-off places, to whom I have said, You are my servant; I chose you, I have not rejected you – Do not fear: I am with you; do not be anxious: I am your God. I will strengthen you, I will help you, I will uphold you with my victorious right hand."* ~Isaiah 41:9-10

REAL LIFE: *"A person who lives in faith must proceed on incomplete evidence, trusting in advance what will only make sense in reverse."*~Philip Yancey

"I have you," God speaks these words to us every day, but how often do we allow ourselves to hear it? Or better yet, how willing are we to allow him to *have* us? Allow me to clarify this phrase. The emphasis is not

on *you,* but is on *have;* it's an offering of support. Furthermore, the phrase is not, *"I had you"* or, *"I will have you."* No, it's in the present because He has us always in everything bad and good. Often, we refuse to hear these words from God because we have chosen to think we are strong enough to go it alone. But when He says, *"I have you"* it's not because we are too weak to go on by ourselves. It's with caring He reminds us we are never left to be by ourselves. This love between God and us is a two-way relationship where He is asking us to accept help in times of need. Our repayment of love should be to give respect and glory to Him when He provides for our requests.

From experience, I can tell you, *"I have you"* is the most comforting and fulfilling phrase you can *feel* God say to you. In times of defeat, He cradles us tight and rocks us, wiping every tear. When we are victorious through our good deeds in the world, He lifts us up and carries us on His shoulders to hold us higher than we could ever be on our own; almost as to say, *"Well done good and faithful servant."* Our humanness has a tendency to downplay the affection God is showing us in our life experiences. We usually don't want to hear *"I have you"* when things are rough because we thrust ourselves into grief and would much rather feel left alone to add to the self pity we can shroud ourselves in. On the other hand, when things are good, His words are drowned out by the thunderous applause we are giving ourselves for what we have accomplished and what we feel entitled to. There are times during various periods of our faith journey, when we try to explain to people what Christ can do for them; in some cases this is not the proper approach. I have realized most often, that people know what He can do for them, it's more of a matter of pointing out to them when He has done these things for them already. We need to continually ask ourselves, "Do I give Him glory when a prayer is answered or He has provided in ways I will never know?" The realization that He never stops *having us* is the first step in understanding how the richness of faith is achieved by recognizing grace at all times. We are constantly in a dilemma of trying to understand the fullness of love God provides through what is next, instead of receiving what is now. At some point we just must trust the mystery of faith, because His love is not measurable nor does it ever end, regardless of who we think we are.

There is one more step to this theory of God holding us at all times. The "unanswered" prayer, or so we think, is also part of the deal. If God truly knows what is best for us, then it might even be that He has us by not granting a self serving request. As children of God, we kick and scream and get bitter when we do not see the fruits of our labor from vigilant prayer. But

I ask any one of you who has ever said "No" to a child, did you do it to be mean or did you do it because you were protecting them? In the moment, it's nearly impossible to recognize when the seemingly lack of a response to our plea was just God focusing on where He was carrying us to next. It goes back to the words the Lord gave to Paul, in 2Corinthians 12:9, *"My grace is sufficient for you, for power is made perfect in weakness."* Paul's acknowledgement is immediate with his words of understanding saying, *"...for when I am weak, then I am strong"* (2Cor 12:10). We apply this to waiting periods in our life which take place where our own insecurities cause weakness; we must transfer our fears into a trust of God's grace and the strength it provides us to overcome all.

In our relationship with Christ, it's critical we allow Him to be both caretaker and cheerleader for us. We are always so crazy being independent and trying to do things on our own, that we do not allow ourselves to be served and supported. Our weakness is understood, it's the reason He came to Earth and died for us. As silly as our problems seem in comparison to others some days, remember, He died for you and had you in His arms while doing it.

Whatever the reason is, stop preventing yourself from recognizing the sound of the beautiful words

Christ is whispering to you, *"I have you today and always."* At times in our life, there are things that just happen when nothing on Earth can heal. He carries us, He walks with us, He talks for us... no matter the circumstance, *He has us.*

I know God had me and still *has me* when... (Name some moments of weakness and some moments of victory)

How can you surrender to God so He can make you strong when you are weak?

Today I will...

Chapter 9

Food for Thought...

FAITH: *"God has made everything appropriate to its time, but has put the timeless into their hearts so they cannot find out, from beginning to end, the work which God has done. I recognized that there is nothing better than to rejoice and to do well during life. Moreover, that all can eat and drink and enjoy the good of all their toil — this is a gift of God." ~Ecclesiastes 3:11-13*

REAL LIFE: *"We must accept finite disappointment, but we must never lose infinite hope."*
~Martin Luther King Jr.

We love our food don't we? As a society, we spend most of our time planning what we are going to eat, where we are going to eat and then we even plan a lot of our lives around when we are going to eat.

Some of the greatest husband and wife arguments of all time have come around the event that provides nourishment to our bodies to sustain life... FOOD! This overall idea makes me take a step back to ask, "Why don't we plan as much time or put as much thought into the spiritual food which will provide us hope, heal our hearts and liven up our soul." After all, the reasons above clearly show when it comes to food for thought, timing is everything.

Depending on the type of food being prepared and all its flavor nuances, we want to feast on it before it either gets cold or warms up to room temperature. We long to experience its texture and tastes before it marinates too long or quite possibly dries out from overcooking; hence, we tend to it like a piece of art. We know the perfect blend of ingredients from the recipe will yield a product fulfilling our palette and cure our hunger. So, we set our tables (or our TV trays) and put everything in place to eat. In the midst of all this, never in a million years would our plan be to do all this prep and then walk away till later or throw the freshly cooked meal in the garbage. So why is it okay when it comes to God?

Just like with our food, faith delivers the same opportunities through God. We are only given a short window to experience necessary gratification, peace or fulfillment based on a specific faith food made to order at that particular instant in time. All of the planning and thought has been handled by God and if we don't use it, the moment passes and the intention is missed. Sure, God will ultimately prepare it for us again, but we will have to wait. We passed on His meal and didn't take advantage while it was at the peak of its goodness. If we believe things have their time and place or that things happen for a reason, then we should fully realize we have to feast *now* on the life situation we are being served. I will say, the dish may not always be what *we* ordered, but we must trust we are served by a Master who knows what will make us stronger and healthier in the long run.

Still fresh in my mind is this vivid replay of our family sitting at the dinner table with my son as he "diplomatically" pleads his case to NOT have to eat the green beans in front of him. I take my role as the stern father who knows best, firmly standing my ground and telling him he needs to eat them because it is necessary for his growing needs and nutrition. I know in my heart, no matter what conversation (a.k.a. argument) takes place, that my son needs to eat some vegetables. After being through this a few hundred times, he knows he will not be allowed to leave the table or continue on to dessert until they are gone. My wife and I are not alone in this endeavor. Almost every parent or babysitter has experienced this in one way or another during their days as a caregiver. Quite honestly, many times it seems like more trouble than it's worth, but it's what is best for the child. Well, welcome to the struggle the Lord has with us every day. Each moment He knows what is needed to sustain us on our journey. We can either choose to take it at the moment we are living, prolong the inevitable or be miserable while doing it; regardless, we still aren't leaving the table until it's over.

Uniquely, our seat at the table means we are required to play dual roles in life as chef and guest while we are being served by the Lord. The food He sends us is also to be shared with others the moment we receive it so it is fresh and at its peak. If we delay in the feast, we can possibly be denying someone else what they are longing to be fed. This means send the card to say, "I love you", pick up the phone to say, "I miss you" or simply offer a smile to a stranger. No matter what the action is, don't wait. The food for thought is really what makes us happy, what allows us to be a friend and what is good within us to help change the world. The meal is us being what God has called us to be.

To me, it does not seem like a coincidence the food pyramid consists of the same outline as the symbol of the Holy Trinity. Our spiritual lives need to only consist of three basic food groups: Father, Son and Holy Spirit. So many times we reach our breaking point and would rather starve ourselves from being fed by prayer and faith, than stepping up to the table to accept what has been prepared for us. We need to say we are hungry and God will provide what is best to enrich us. Concentrate on what is at your place and on your plate; do not let it go bad while you focus on what is missing. With the same conviction you worry about how many omega 3's you took in today, stop and pray about how much you can be filled up by a healthy dose of the "Alpha and Omega."

How am I dining with the Lord or how am I stepping away from what has been prepared for me?

In what ways can I remain at "the table" and accept the nourishment I am being offered?

Today I will…

Chapter 10

I Once Could See, but Now I'm Blind...

<u>FAITH</u>: *"Consider it all joy, my brothers, when you encounter various trials, for you know that the testing of your faith produces perseverance. And let perseverance be perfect, so that you may be perfect and complete, lacking in nothing."* ~James 1:2-4

<u>REAL LIFE</u>: *"A man of character finds a special attractiveness in difficulty, since it is only by coming to grips with difficulty that he can realize his potentialities."* ~Charles De Gaule

The last line from the opening phrase of *'Amazing Grace'* is sung emphatically, "...was blind, but now, I see," but how do we address our faith journey when our once unshakable devotion becomes uprooted?

Devastatingly, the words we once sang with hope somehow become reversed and we realize, "...we once could see, but now are blind."

Each day people struggle with adversities, which take them from the picturesque surroundings of God's grace to a dark place with no sense of direction. The light of living out the commitments of their beliefs fades into darkness, blinding them to forget about the things that once grounded them. How are people dealing with overcoming the ultimate crisis that has shaken their faith? How are you overcoming burnout in a relationship, job or situation which no longer fulfills you the way it once did? These are not easy questions, but you mustn't lose sight of what you desire to a temporary darkness that can be healed. It takes work and devotion, but you can, and will, be brought back to the state of light in which all was clear to you; if you seek it.

In Mark 8:22-26 we learn of a blind man who is healed by Jesus, but within this passage the man is not healed by Jesus' first attempt to cure him. After Christ wipes His saliva on the man's eyes, he can see only blurred people who *"look like trees."* This is a rare instance where we hear in scripture of a person not being healed at the moment Jesus goes to work. In this encounter, it takes a second wipe of spittle from the

Savior before his vision is completely restored. The word *"restored"* implies a belief the man could once see, but lost his ability somewhere along the way. Our own lives are very much the same as this man. We want to be able to believe long enough to see grace in the world around us, however most times we need a second round of strong reassurance from God before it becomes clear. Even deeper, as human beings we must be aware, sometimes God's reassurance alone is not enough; we must be open enough to allow His grace to navigate our course.

It's important for us to understand what it means to trust in God at all costs. We should be hopeful, realizing a change from the light to the dark does not have to be permanent in any situation. Many different events and circumstances can be contributing factors causing us to doubt in the darkest of days. It must be our desire to re-ground ourselves after our own fears have caused us to lose sight; if we let it, this level of fear will own us and no longer allow us to be fulfilled. It's necessary to know God's plan is designed for our own humanness to get in the way, causing delays along the path. Our role is to fall back on our trust in God to overcome this temporary blindness and allow His guidance to put us back on the track of fulfilling our ultimate purpose in this life.

From my own experiences, I can tell you one of the scariest feelings in the world is to doubt what you believe, even for the briefest of moments. We fall so hard and so fast from the "mountain top" which allowed us to see the landscape of all God has in store for us. When we finally land, we wind up in a pitch black cavern filled with the loneliness of despair that seems irreversible.

You may be someone who is just finding your faith, someone who has not allowed yourself to surrender or someone who has forgotten what it was like to experience grace at all. Any of these types of blindness are just as curable within you and your desire to seek God. There must be a release from the crutches we utilize to create a false form of vision which tells us things can never be any better. The redeeming news for all of us is, at the deepest core of our faith is Christ. He remains present always; to restore our sight should we choose to implore Him to do so. Do not be discouraged in your blindness; simply accept the gifts in front of you to bring back your vision and accept nothing less than complete vision.

Take a moment of prayer to surrender your fears, faults, failures, vices and all things that have power over us robbing you of your sight. To be able to see is not just an appearance of objects; it is trust in the truth, seeing all things as they are intended to be seen. The beauty of life is in front of you, today is for you to enjoy. Lay your struggles at the foot of the cross and allow Christ to rub His saliva on your eyes once more.

What is it that I long to see?

What are the pitfalls that have clouded my vision or have prevented me from recognizing all that is good?

Today I will...

Chapter 11

Tom and Jerry...

FAITH: *"So turn from youthful desires and pursue righteousness, faith, love, and peace, along with those who call on the Lord with purity of heart. Avoid foolish and ignorant debates, for you know that they breed quarrels." ~2Timothy 2:22-23*

REAL LIFE: *"The most important trip you may take in life is meeting people half way." ~Henry Boyle*

While watching my children go at it as only siblings can, I had this vivid flashback to that classic cartoon *Tom and Jerry*. At that moment, it was as if I was sitting in a room staring at a television screen at those two animated adversaries. Instead of a mouse and a cat, I had two competitive children constantly pushing each other's buttons until some sort of brutal retaliation occurred. One poked, one bonked the other and then they ran around the house yelling gibberish which resembled the sound effects Hanna Barbera and MGM Studios utilize.

The physical needling, and at times comical groans, is not where the similarity of these rivals ends. Much like my children, at the end of the day, Tom and Jerry really never had a problem with each other. It wasn't ever clear in the seventeen years of cartoons why Tom (the cat) chases Jerry (the mouse); after all he does catch him every once in a while but never eats him. As a matter of fact, in some episodes, the duo actually works together for the common good. It is a love-hate relationship of competition simply for the sake of competition. This is what can happen when we stop competing for one another and begin to battle against each other.

In life and faith, we chase the unattainable and every once in a while God answers our prayers and we get what we want. The problem is, when we get it, we really do not know what to do with it. The chase is over and we look back and see the prize would have been nothing without the pursuit. Likewise, if you took either Tom or Jerry out of the mix, the other would be empty or lost; their sense of purpose and drive would seem to fade. A situation of them journeying alone would leave them defeated even in their own ultimate victory.

In the same manner, our faith is like a game of cat and mouse. It is a never-ending contest in which we struggle to always test what we believe. We want to challenge the rituals, customs and scriptures. We look to downplay the everyday miracles that occur as crazy or strange occurrences. We live our lives with a holier than thou attitude, criticizing those around us who do not display the same core values we do. We are the ones creating our own inner struggle, derailing us from our intended purpose. All the while, God plays His role by not intervening and letting free-will determine which path we take. He knows, if we truly believe, we will run back to Him because it's impossible to know true fulfillment without Him. We must embrace times when our faith challenges us to know it is for our benefit. Even in *Tom and Jerry,* it always concluded with a handshake of the two rivals. It was an affirmation they knew it really is about *the chase* more than it is about the outcome of a competition between two supposed rivals.

So it goes in my house after all the arguing and fighting of my children. When the dust settles and quiet visits our home again, I take a peek in my son's bedroom to see there was no referee needed, no life lesson to be taught, just a brother and sister cuddling in the same bed reading a book together. All this allows me to know they understand, because in the end, they have the same goals in mind and deep in their hearts they love each other unconditionally. My only advice with this scenario in mind is: Take life's obstacles as part of the journey. Although, never forget that what you ultimately seek would not be the same if there was no one, or nothing there in your path, to challenge and nudge you along during the journey.

Describe/Name a love-hate relationship in your life you can work on to allow respect to shine through more constantly.

When have you recognized your faith at work and then downplayed it as mere coincidence or entitlement?

Today I will...

Chapter 12

Compete Well...

FAITH: *"For I am not ashamed of the gospel. It is the power of God for the salvation of everyone who believes: for Jew first, and then Greek. For in it is revealed the righteousness of God from faith to faith; as it is written, 'The one who is righteous by faith will live.'"*
~Romans 1:16-17

REAL LIFE: *"You may have to fight a battle more than once to win it."* *~Margaret Thatcher*

In August of 2011, Hurricane Irene wreaked havoc along the East Coast of the United States. My wife, Aimee, took some time off work to go assist with some of the cleanup in New Jersey. She rallied friends to bring cleaning supplies and we re-arranged our schedules so I could take care of our own children while she was away. Her spirit was strong in knowing what she had to do and where she needed to be. When Aimee arrived though, she was not prepared for how fresh the shock of the events were for those who lived there and had lost nearly everything. In the wake of the disaster one man cried out, "Where is your God now? Where is God in this?" These statements brought a deep sadness to Aimee being the faithful woman she is; after all, she was there because of God and His call. Well, within one day, God answered the questions of that man. An aid van full of workers looking to help in any way came to town and stopped near the home where Aimee was helping. Their clean-up efforts were done with joy, with compassion and with a labor that saved the family tens of thousands of dollars in cleanup money. When she called to tell me the story, I knew how it would end when she first started speaking. Even though the questioning of God's presence brought sorrow to my heart, I knew how easy the answer is for those who question where God is: "He is in the rescuers, He is in the Red Cross volunteers going without sleep so others have food and shelter, and He is in those sending donations to help lighten the affected burdens." The home my wife helped save that week was rebuilt and the family now lives in it again...dare I say with a God who is also there, whether they choose to recognize Him or not.

In a life of constant struggle, we could say God has left us alone any time we face adversity. But the truth is, He is always just competing for a way to let us know He is in the World around us, right by the side of the faithful. He begs for our attention and will keep coming to us in different ways, trying and trying until we recognize Him. Some will refuse to recognize Him, while others will weep in His presence. Those who believe God walks with us, answer the call placed on their hearts to recognize Him and fight for what they know is truth.

Our role as Christians is to go out into the world and be the answer in the cries of the helpless and fight to be the living example of Christ to others. I once again am drawn to the powerful lines St. Paul writes in 1Timothy 6:12, *"Compete well for the faith..."* Paul is not just telling us to be passive and just have faith when it is convenient. His choice of words does not say, "Well if things are good, maybe I'll have faith" or, "Today you might want to show people where your beliefs are." He instead uses the word *"compete" to* let us know there are days we will have to fight for what we believe. This battle is not just about the words we choose to use saying, "We believe," it's about the manner in which we are the living example of what being a child of God means. It will not always be comfortable, but it should remain a loving example of community, harmony and conviction of what is possible through Christ.

A life of faith is an *all-the-time* gig. This means we have to pray when things are good as well as bad. Our prayers should not just be a lament; then we look like a bunch of complainers never getting what we want. Our prayers must also be to find the good in what we are given by God for the times He comes to us "with skin on," present as a human in the works of others who care for us; then we pray in thanksgiving in the same manner. Football players don't only compete when they are losing a game, but they work to keep the lead when they are winning the contest as well. Let your faith life set the example for those who look to you for inspiration. Allow others to see that you cherish what you have and how it makes you compete well for the faith, in praise and desperation.

Competing well for the faith is not just to show others we are good people; it is to put God's love into their hearts in a manner that allows their own faith to grow over time. Take time to not only pray a, "Thank you" for what you have, but more importantly, relax in the moment to pick another person to pray for. If in addition to offering up our own needs, we find the good in the day and lift up prayers for those around us, the focus and the burden is lifted off what we do not have and becomes more about what we are blessed with. Compete well not only for yourself, but for those who need it even more.

How do you see it?

*GOD IS **NOWHERE***

*GOD IS **NOW** HERE*

Do you always *compete well* for the faith? How and Why?

Name ways you can work to show a deeper commitment for what you believe.

Today I will…

Chapter 13

Take Time for Yourself...

FAITH: *"The LORD is my shepherd; there is nothing I lack. In green pastures he makes me lie down; to still waters he leads me; he restores my soul. He guides me along right paths for the sake of his name."*
~Psalms 23:1-3

REAL LIFE: *"In three words I can sum up everything I've learned about life... it goes on."* *~Robert Frost*

Sometimes in life we need a public service announcement to draw our attention to important messages. Taking time for yourself is definitely one of those messages. Many times we find ourselves making out work schedules or family schedules and in the process we realize we have completely filled most days with "things to do." For instance, our summer family activities begin to go on the calendar at the end of spring, but we are smacked in the face when it shows by the time all the already planned activities are put on the calendar, summer will be over and the kids are back in school. We sit back and are bummed because at that point they hadn't even gotten out yet! This type of insight can cause us great anxiety. It also pushes us into a bigger issue, when will we find a way to take time for ourselves?

The mere notion of having to take time for me is way too selfish for me to comprehend. This theory is one that has been advised over and over again by those who are much wiser, so I go with trying to make it a priority. The truth behind it is, if we are on empty, we can no longer be a quality version of ourselves. Without a refreshed mind and body, we are just wandering around aimlessly, missing all that is going on in the wonderful world around us. The theory is no different than what they tell us during safety instructions on an airplane, "Put the oxygen mask on yourself first and then assist those around you." We must be able to play our role for others around us, but without having life within us, it's not possible.

Taking time for yourself does not just involve running errands and watching television to turn off your brain (although sometimes it does help to alleviate stress). You need to find something to stimulate your mind and re-energize you. This type of restoration is about you being all you can be by finding things which inspire you, allowing you to take notice of who you want to be. A self-offered getaway from reality means to break away from meaningless conversation and gossip, so you can put a focus on positive discussions of encouragement. You may even end up turning off your cell phone when in the car, so you can use quiet time to drive and spiritually reflect on personal growth.

Even the Son of God knew when it was time to get away and recharge His batteries. These are the moments we read about in the Bible. For instance, in Luke 5:15-16, *"...great crowds assembled to listen to him and to be cured of their ailments, but he would withdraw to deserted places to pray."* Again in Matthew 14:23, right before He is about to walk on the water, *"...he went up on the mountain by himself to pray. When it was evening he was there alone."* His mission was of the people and for His people, but often the crowds became too large and His focus was lost. His faithfulness allowed Him to know when it was time to re-center His being and offer prayer back to His Father. Renewed in the Spirit, He would return and jump right back into the work necessary for Him to do.

So many things in the world prevent us from being present in the moment. Without viewing our current situations and relationships in life from a renewed perspective, we can lose ourselves. It becomes impossible to satisfy anyone else if we do not have the fuel to be the person others need us to be. An unclear mind overwhelms us, drawing attention to what is not being done and focusing on what we have zero control over. The need for you to take time for yourself is not a suggestion, it's a demand others who love you will respect. If you are only giving those you care about ten percent of you, most likely they see and feel you are giving them nothing at all. So here is the question of this moment, "What are you doing for yourself today?" Whatever it is, allow yourself to be committed and present in the moment.

*If you are going to your child's sports event or production at school...*Watch it and recognize they will only be this young once. Your being there is a sign of support they long for.

If you are going to a family get together... Remind yourself you do not get to choose your family and you probably seem as crazy to them as they seem to you. Above all, appreciate that you have a family.

If you are taking a vacation... Worry less about where you have to be or what you have to do that day and absorb the surroundings you can't always geographically take advantage of.

If you are praying, then "pray"... fall into the conversation with God you need to have, so He may help you become all you desire to be.

How do you feel after you have taken "real" *time for yourself* and why?

When have you missed major opportunities to be in the moment?

Today I will...

Chapter 14

Who's Your Simon?...

FAITH: *"What good is it, my brothers, if someone says he has faith but does not have works? Can that faith save him? If a brother or sister has nothing to wear and has no food for the day, and one of you says to them, "Go in peace, keep warm, and eat well," but you do not give them the necessities of the body, what good is it? So also faith of itself, if it does not have works, is dead."* ~James 2:14-17

REAL LIFE: *"People see God every day, they just don't recognize him."* ~Pearl Bailey

"I quit, I cannot do this anymore!" is a phrase that has leapt from my lips in the most desperate moments of personal struggle. Whether it's with our faith, career, or even in the tough spots of relationships, this

is a cry for help the Lord understands; though He knows it is not coming from our hearts, but our heads. Within love and commitment there is passion for what we believe. Even though we know what we are doing is right, we sometimes grow fatigued from the weight of what is placed on our shoulders. For me, I may have those days or moments where I get tired of fighting on and that is when a *"Simon"* is placed in my life to allow me to carry on. So, let me ask you, "Who's Your Simon today or where has he been present lately?"

"As they led him away they took hold of a certain Simon, a Cyrenian, who was coming in from the country; and after laying the cross on him, they made him carry it behind Jesus" (Luke 23:26). Ultimately, Jesus Christ was true God and true man; He did not need anyone to help him carry His cross, nor was He going to ask. Despite this fact, a man named *Simon* was taken from the crowd to bear the load and ensure Jesus would not collapse prior to reaching His final destination. What *Simon* represented in that moment wasn't just about being a commoner created to handle extra weight for Jesus. For me, Simon represents all of humanity. Each day, we encounter opportunities where we either need a *Simon* to help us along or we are called to be *Simon* for someone else who is struggling with their own cross.

At first, the crucifixion journey didn't include Simon at all while he stood watching from the sea of people; it was neither his problem nor his cross to carry. Yet, (whether you believe he did it willingly or was forced to do it) he looked upon Jesus' frailness, grabbed the wood and walked with him because an innocent man was facing torment no human should endure. Simon shows us we must go beyond what we want to do and do what is absolutely necessary. After all who really wants to carry someone else's cross?

We can also look at this from a different angle and survey it from our perspective in how we acknowledge help as well. Christ's willingness to accept Simon's assistance shows incredible humility. This example teaches us that even while approaching His final moments, Christ was allowing someone else to begin being His hands and feet on this Earth. In a way, it shows we should not be too proud to accept assistance in the most desperate of moments while fulfilling our purpose.

Often we question, "Why?" but really we should be asking, "Who or what are You sending, Lord, to get me through this difficulty I face?" There is a *Simon* around the corner who will be there for you when you feel you can no longer go on. But like Christ, will you allow him to carry your cross?

We live in a society that can encourage us to always take care of ourselves first, but this level of thinking causes us to be self absorbed with our own issues. We miss out on opportunities of service that can make the world a better place. If we focus on our own journey or our own cross too long, without accepting assistance from those sent to help us, then we will miss the times we are being plucked from the crowd in order to carry the cross for someone else. Who are we to think it is not our job to carry the cross for our brothers and sisters? We must be in this together, working as one body of Christ to help one another along.

Remember, the body of Christ is made up of all those who were part of His story, as well as those who are part of our story. Just like you, Simon's role that day was bigger than anyone could have foreseen. I cannot imagine the pride and honor Simon might have held in his heart for the privilege of carrying the Messiah's cross. We need to view opportunities when we are called to take another's strife into our own hands and help them journey as a privilege.

I invite you to look around in all instances and recognize who is being sent to help... "Who's your

Simon?" Each day Christ is present in the *Simon* sent to us to be our helper, to be the one to carry our crosses when life is at its toughest. Once you feel strong enough, return the favor just as Christ did through his resurrection and be *Simon* for someone else. After all, when you really get to the heart of the matter, the cross Jesus carried to Calvary that day was not His own, but it was for our sins... and He did it for *all* of us.

Who was my *Simon* this day and how did they help carry the load on my shoulders?

Have I missed opportunities to serve others that have a harder journey than I at the moment? How can I change it?

Today I will...

Chapter 15

The Last I Love You…

FAITH: *"Your every act should be done with love."* ~1Corinthians 16:14

REAL LIFE: *"As we express our gratitude, we must never forget that the highest appreciation is not to utter words, but to live by them." ~John F. Kennedy*

Sometimes when I get into a busy stretch or involved in a work related project, I can forget about many of the things and people I hold so dear. All of us need to stop ourselves periodically and reflect for a few minutes each day on what we cherish and the way in which we share our appreciation for others. When we get caught up in the "busyness" of life, it can mean we miss out on things very important to us and those around us. We are never promised tomorrow and our impact is meant for today; opportunities that exist now could vanish in an instant and any "I love you" could be the last "I love you" to someone we care about.

Now don't let this become about some dark reminder of our mortality, but rather a challenge that helps make us better friends and turns the world into a better place. I understand how hard it is to live every day as if we are dying when reality creeps in and we are caught up in life. However, I also know each one of us can stop and say a simple, "I love you," just in case.

In my home, we have a rule: you are under no circumstance allowed to go to bed without telling each person in the house you love them. Even if we have argued or allowed the anxieties of tomorrow to overwhelm us, we must take a moment to say those feelings will pass but we are family and we love at all costs. For me, I try carrying it through into all my relationships making an attempt to empty myself each day by saying too much to those I appreciate, rather than to miss out and live the rest of my life never having said enough. My friends know I wear my heart on my sleeve, good and bad. Each of them knows how true it is that I need to make sure they are aware of just how special they are.

In the same way, the notion of being aware to never take anything for granted can be adhered to in prayer. What were your last words in prayer today? Were you busy complaining? Are you praying for something to change? For forgiveness? Are you grateful for what you have? Have you simply told God, "I love you" lately and "Thank you" for what you have, and what you have been protected from? We prepare each day for what is next, but are we pausing to just say "I love you" and sincerely show it when we walk away from each person we value? The answers really to these questions are our ultimate prayer back to Him. *"For God so loved the world that he gave his only Son"* (John 3:16). The least we can do is to show respect and appreciation for that gift.

My friend Steve Angrisano once said he would like to replace all the places it says "love" in the Bible with the words, "ultimate respect." Because love is more than just a word, it is about everything it stands for, saying, "I will be there and have your back always." I now use this phrase often in the closing of emails and letters to friends to express how valuable they are and as a sign of respect for what they mean to me. So, remember to take a few seconds and show those you care for the best possible sign of ultimate respect with a heartfelt, hopeful, last "I Love You."

Let the realization and power of this phrase be the reminder to give that extra smile, share an extra laugh, hug tighter and apologize even if it is not your fault. Make sure everyone you care about gets their last "I Love You" and pray with gratefulness as a sign of adoration and not a literal good bye. Remember though, if doing this with ultimate respect, it has to be more than an implied smile; it must be a blend of resonating words and actions which provide comfort today and always. It's my hope if everyone who reads this does just that, we have all begun to do our part to change the world. In this spirit, as a child of God, I say to you, "I love you."

Have I told everyone I care for today that I love them? If not, who do I need to make that extra effort to let them know I care and how will I do this?

What are ways I can go beyond words this day to show love?

Today I will...

Chapter 16

You Duped Me...

FAITH: *"Trust in the LORD with all your heart, on your own intelligence do not rely; In all your ways be mindful of him, and he will make straight your paths."*
~*Proverbs 3:5-6*

REAL LIFE: *"Perseverance is the hard work you do after you get tired of doing the hard work you already did."*
~*Newt Gingrich*

"If it was easy everyone would do it," is how the old saying goes. Anyone who has fought for what they believe in beyond approval, or even quite possibly their own understanding, can relate to this message. Every now and then though, we are just plain tired of life being hard and ultimately feel *duped*. This happens either by our own thinking being persuaded by others, or sometimes it seems by the very faith we put our trust in.

I love the book of Jeremiah from the Hebrew Scriptures for many reasons. He and I seem to have a connection of feeling unworthy. At first to be called to proclaim God's word and eventually giving in, only to then have it out with the Heavenly Father who "hired" us on. I believe anyone who has trusted beyond sight or understanding shares moments of frustration when life isn't going our way. The illustration in Jeremiah 20:7 accurately depicts the moments of rejection that make us question God's plan: *"You duped me, O LORD, and I let myself be duped; you were too strong for me, and you triumphed. All the day I am an object of laughter; everyone mocks me."* At this point in scripture, Jeremiah is lost, angry and defeated because of the negative focus others are putting on him as a result of his beliefs and the message he works to share. However, what he goes on to say just two verses later, is pure faith driven realization. Despite his lamenting, the prophet continues on with one of the most powerful verses in this entire book, *"I say to myself, I will not mention him, I will speak in his name no more. But then it becomes like fire burning in my heart, imprisoned in my bones; I grow weary holding it in, I cannot endure it"* (Jeremiah 20:9). This duped prophet is basically proclaiming, despite all the pain and ridicule God's Word brings him, he cannot hold it in because he knows what is true and real! For me, this provides hope and reassurance for those times in our lives we spend living our faith, only to have one in ten people willing to recognize Christ within us. Once you know the feeling of what it's like to just change one life, you wouldn't trade it for the world.

Within being humble we sometimes feel like others (or even God) have gotten the best of us. We continue on to think, "How could God allow this to happen to those following him?" All I can tell you is it's part of the call and we endure for the rewards it yields. We must persevere and not give up, because even Christ was subject to ridicule and suffering in His own life. Why would we think our journey would not be filled with tests and bumps along the way? We strive to be Christ in the world and model the same steps He walked, steps that did not give up. No matter the relationship or situation, at some point there will be a time you'll feel you just want to flat out throw it all away. Not wanting to go on because of adversity causes you to question "the plan" that is truly best for you. Jeremiah knew that feeling too, but we are only given the inspiration and gift through his words. He chose to recognize his call and convey the message he was blessed with for all generations because he recognized how great the grace of God is.

The danger in any moment we feel duped to the point of giving up is really not about us disappointing God; it's about us being robbed of real happiness in our own life. We certainly can apply this level of thinking regardless of our passion or lifelong dreams; we will always experience moments of fatigue or betrayal leaving us weak. This mindset then results in us feeling trapped, causing us not just to deny Jesus, but to deny ourselves. Our ambitions will get lost and not following them could be our emotional demise. However, reaching this breaking point while rooted in faith is not all bad. When we see things from a hurt perspective, we humble ourselves to allow God's true will for us to be our light. At this time, we will allow Him to take over our being to the point in which His goodness springs forth into the world. It will bring about the same realization that our commitment is blessed in the manner similar to the way Jeremiah reassures how true surrender to God turns out, "...*the LORD is with me, like a mighty champion: my persecutors will stumble, they will not prevail... LORD of hosts, you test the just, you see mind and heart...*" (Jeremiah 20:11-12).

Don't be ashamed of your own inner struggles, embrace them. Every once in a while God wants you to question your role on Earth and then fight for what you know is truth. God grants you free will hoping you use the gift of wisdom to determine if you are truly on the right path and then work to follow it faithfully. We can relate to Jeremiah because in his lashing outs, he shows his own humanness. In my own life, I have trusted and followed the Lord's plan for me to a point in which those around me viewed my decisions as "irresponsible." I always know He will provide, and I know He will not let me fail because He has shown me time and time again His reward. Sure, the faithful do experience tough times because of their beliefs and their "faithfully irresponsible" approach of knowing God wins in the end. However, once you experience the tremendous graces that come along with the victories in God's will are evident, the words, "You duped me," me will never cross your mind again. Life will become about the endurance of faith rather than a sprint for what you desire.

Name a time you felt abandoned by your beliefs.

In times of feeling *duped* or shunned by people close to you, have you ever been able to look back and see growth by noticing it was eventually for the best?

Today I will...

Chapter 17

Take a Chance on Someone...

FAITH: *"And the king will say to them in reply, 'Amen, I say to you, whatever you did for one of these least brothers of mine, you did for me.'"* ~Matthew 25:40

REAL LIFE: *"Why not go out on a limb? Isn't that where the fruit is?"* ~Frank Scully

Sometimes we must turn our focus to redemption. Not only for our own relationship with God, but in ways we can help make a difference for others. People need us to take a chance on them at work, in our friendships, with our family and just in the everyday community. You may need to lower your walls to make yourself vulnerable for the benefit of others. With this kind of openness, you are able to take a chance on that person no one else does. The mere action of risk creates the ability to offer an immeasurable gift, with the power to change a life, through one simple action of belief in another human; it's the only way some people can grow.

Jesus took a chance on twelve young men who knew nothing about ministry; better yet, He relied on them to spread His word for all mankind. He saw in them what no one else could see. Even now, isn't this what God does for us every day? He takes chance after chance that we will be good stewards of all the gifts He bestows upon us. He takes a chance each time we are forgiven for our actions in the hope we will learn from our mistakes and appreciate this redemption. He is ultimately the one who has to clean up our messes. Conversely, remind yourself that sometimes it's necessary to have the courage and strength to let someone take a chance on you because you need it as well.

Knowing that each person, in one way or another is put into our life for a specific reason is the first step. The second is understanding that it's not always because we need them, but that they need us. This theory became very evident in my own life one day while deciding whether or not to go to a spiritual presentation being held at a neighboring church. I told my pastor I would not be there because, as I put it, "I'm not going to get anything out of it and I really don't feel like going to make any new friends." (This quickly became one of those moments as an adult where someone you respect looks at you the same way your parent did when you were a child and you had just talked back to them.) Instantly, he stopped me dead in my tracks, looked me right in the eye and said, "Maybe you think you don't need to be there, but maybe someone else needs you to be there for them; everything is not always about you." He was 100% right, and sheepishly I apologized. So I went, not for my own reasons, but for the purpose which God had in mind for me. Joyfully I was able to be the light of Christ for some people who needed to hear my story that day. Just another reminder, the results may not always be what you want but they are capable of producing great things.

So many people have taken a chance on me throughout my whole life and created opportunities I will never be able to repay them for. In looking at it now, I'm grateful not really for what they did, but just that they were open enough to take a chance on me. It humbles me to know they have such tremendous faith in me as a person, so because of that I strive to never let them down. Just like many people we have all encountered along the way, many of them will never truly know the impact they had in shaping us into who we are today.

When we sacrifice, it is vital we recognize that it's not always about what we give up, but what we can really do for others. God is not going to send you directly to Heaven because you gave up a few indulgences during Lent one year, but He will because, *"you did things for the least of his people"* (Mt 25:40). Take a chance on someone today and be open to God's design. It is essential we let go and make ourselves smaller in order to stop trying to be bigger than God and His will. Through all the good deeds we do for each other, our hearts will be opened and exposed to the unending grace of our Lord. We are to give as much as we receive and the only way we can change the world is together. I love the words in the prayer the "Litany of Humility" as they can definitely be a mantra for helping us focus on others more than ourselves. The prayer ends with the following words, and I pray for my life and yours, we are *"granted the grace to desire it:"*

"That others may be loved more than I...
That others may be esteemed more than I ...
That, in the opinion of the world,
others may increase and I may decrease ...
That others may be chosen and I set aside ...
That others may be praised and I unnoticed ...
That others may be preferred to me in everything...
That others may become holier than I, provided that I
may become as holy as I should... "

Who have you taken a chance on? How did you do it and how did they change?

Who has given you an opportunity or saw more inside you to help you achieve success? What was the contributing factor which changed you?

Today I will...

Chapter 18

Wholly vs. Holy...

FAITH: *"Now may the God of peace Himself sanctify you entirely; and may your spirit and soul and body be preserved complete, without blame at the coming of our Lord Jesus Christ."* ~1Thessalonians 5:23

REAL LIFE: *"Faith is deliberate confidence in the character of God whose ways you may not understand at the time."* ~Oswald Chambers

A man sits on the curb after losing his job and struggles to accept the reality that he is unemployed. He looks to the sky and blurts out, "How could you do this to me? I am a holy man who tries my best! Am I not good enough to be worthy?" What this hurt soul doesn't know is, the Lord does see him as a holy man and is simply looking to reward him. This dedicated servant was stuck in the position at his job and was not being utilized to the best of his ability. His talents were being lost and not shared properly. It became necessary for God to intervene which caused temporary emptiness in an attempt to lift the man up to another level of faithfulness and make him *wholly*. The man's happiness, and purpose, is dependent upon surrendering to God's will, which places him in a career he will excel in. At this moment, he begins to write a new chapter of his life where he is made whole.

These situations happen all the time where we become trapped and stop working towards fulfilling our purpose. God knows we grow weak in our humanness during certain periods of confrontation between the spiritual grace we desire and the physical insecurities our world delivers. Complacency in a situation will cause us to settle for less than we deserve; God gets involved to save us. We can also be robbed of the wonderful gifts we possess if we remain involved too long in a spot where we are being hurt. The Lord longs to remove us from suffering and into a place where healing can begin, whether we actually recognize the need for it or not. He sees the part of us that is missing or lost. Sometimes, it's a key component of our genetic make-up which is stolen; leaving us incomplete. Without being *wholly* unified, we cannot be *holy* in a manner conducive to the person we long to be.

   Wholly is a different level of growth in our faith which allows us into a deeper realization of where God is at work. It is a step beyond *holy* where we become submerged in our trust in the Lord. In order for us to be open and completely spiritual, we must relieve ourselves of the reservations and human desires which allow negative thoughts of self worth to consume us. Our faith walk will eventually reach a point in which we can honestly say we are *wholly* one with God.

   In this debate of *Wholly vs. Holy*, a new height of living moves us past an understanding of what the different spelling of these two words really mean. For example, *holy* takes you to mass or worship, *wholly* is submerging yourself in prayer to think of God's will beyond your own immediate wants. *Holy* sends a check to the local charity, *wholly* takes your family to a local soup kitchen to serve and dine with those who have nothing. *Holy* is a great start to being faithful and knowing you want to serve God, but it is when we are *wholly*, we begin to meet God in all things and all people. I'm not asking you to read into this and think being *holy* in all these instances is not enough. Doing His will is more than enough. *Wholly* is just a fullness of offering all you are made of back to God, which may be harder than we like at times. Our concentration when we pray to those who have gone before us living a saintly life should be to comprehend we are praying for their *wholly-ness* more than their *holiness*. Those revered as saints, risked more than they needed to in order to live their lives of faith and we look up to them for that.

All of this really comes to light when we feel that we are unworthy for God's grace. We become bogged down feeling unworthy of His love or drown in pity thinking He has given up on us. What it should be is a call to form a deeper relationship so our commitment to Him is as great as His commitment to us, reassurance we walk together. Scripture refers to the church as His "bride;" it reminds us of the faithfulness the Lord seeks to have with us. He wants to celebrate our bond with a feast like no other. *Wholly* communion allows us to dine with, not only Christ, but also each and every member of our community of believers who make up the faith community. Deeper yet, our responsibility within this community helps us make decisions to give of ourselves completely in adoration of the Bridegroom.

Don't let *holy* become a goal which requires us to analyze every human action we make. Offer yourself *wholly* to allow God to do what He does best when working through us. If we have offered up all we are, we begin to see the bigger picture of where our life is headed. We can look back at our past events and see every facet where we have been provided for. We see God has guided us to a place far beyond what we thought happiness was. After all, when we are *wholly* committed to our faith, aren't we really saying, "I believe at all costs and trust completely?"

When were there times I may have missed God's grace because I was concentrating on being "holy", instead of allowing Him to be "wholly" one with me?

Name some experiences when struggle actually brought you closer to God and deeper in faith...

Today I will…

Chapter 19

Stop Searching...

FAITH: *"Have no anxiety at all, but in everything, by prayer and petition, with thanksgiving, make your requests known to God. Then the peace of God that surpasses all understanding will guard your hearts and minds in Christ Jesus." ~Philippians 4:6-7*

REAL LIFE: *"The only true wisdom is in knowing you know nothing." ~Socrates*

Have you ever had one of those conversations where someone is telling you everything they desire for their future? You know what I mean, a good, long, life giving exhortation encompassing all they want to journey towards in life. However, you realize the whole time, while the words are coming out of their mouth, they are really answering their own questions. Even better yet, are you the one searching for solutions eluding you, but the solutions you are finding seem way too simple? Most of the times when others seek us out or we confide in others, it is not really that they need our advice or we need theirs. The person on the other end simply is there as the sounding board. We need to find comfort as we verbalize our desires (or fears) in a manner relating to where we are in life. It's in conversations such as these we sometimes gloss over the fact God has provided answers for us through our own resolve. As a matter of fact, quite often we are all guilty of not recognizing that the answer to our prayer is not hidden at all, but rather within our reach at this very moment. The catch is, because it's not difficult enough to find, we continue on our search. We must stop searching!

In a world where everything is at our fingertips and we want an answer NOW! We Google it, ask Siri, plug it in our Garmin or simply call 411 for information and instantaneously we get results. To further feed our need for timely answers, we even get a myriad of options to choose from. Compounding this overload of results, we immediately begin to scroll through possible remedies so fast, we blow right past the one that has all the information we desire. So what do you think happens in our own life when we are overwhelmed? In seeking answers, we may get desperate and open up by turning to prayer; that's a good answer. The catch is, without the gratification of instantaneous results, we do not wait for a true response only God can provide. We move on too quickly and we miss what He has put right in front of us while we keep searching. We treat the timing of faithfulness with the same warp speed the Internet offers and throw out prayers like we are putting a phrase into a search engine. Our expectation of finding the answer somewhere down towards the bottom of the page, rather than right in front of us, carries forward in our hopes and desires from God. When the answer is not there instantaneously (or we have missed it), we ask the same question again, except we change the wording. Once again, God provides the answer but we blow right past it; we don't want to spend the time looking in the most obvious place. This all reminds me of when we were kids and would ask questions of the "Magic 8 Ball;" if we didn't like the answer, we'd shake it again. Our spirituality is affected by the world around us and to easily sum it up, "Our prayer life can be more like a sign of the times rather than a sign of the cross."

Matthew 7:7-8 gives us the model in which

faithfulness is fulfilled and grace is granted. Very simply it says, *"Ask and it will be given to you; seek and you will find; knock and the door will be opened to you. For everyone who asks, receives; and the one who seeks, finds; and to the one who knocks, the door will be opened."* This is not a game show. He is asking us to knock and accept what is behind door #1 because He is providing what is best for us. It's not our job to panic and frantically knock on as many doors as possible. Simply stop searching and knock on the door you know can provide you with what you seek, not on all the ones which merely provide temporary satisfaction. I am as guilty as the next person of not offering up patience in order to get an answer to my prayer and so many times I walk away before God can answer it. Even in this case, He is a gracious and loving God who provides grace even when we walk away. He answers our prayer and then leaves it on our front porch like a UPS package waiting for us when we return. It's simply our job to sign for it and accept it.

Once the answer is in our presence, how do we know what to do next or if the response we have gotten is the final answer? Well, there isn't one specific way the solution is provided. The stepping stones of opportunities are there to inspire us as much as they are to fulfill us; each scenario or response from God must be seen through all the way. For instance, the job opportunity that arises and then falls apart doesn't mean failure was supposed to be your destiny, but it does show you courage to go where your heart truly wants to be. The romantic date you go on doesn't have to be one culminating in marriage, but it can show you love in a way that assures you there are other good people in the world. We live and we learn through the noise that exists around us and it is vital we have a "Center" Who can provide us with inner peace to know we are taken care of.

Stop searching for what is already at your feet. When you close your eyes and open your minds to all of your surroundings, you will feel the presence of reassurance and contentment if you let it in. Time, coupled with perseverance, brings the Spirit's living water into our lives, providing us with what we need to live.

Have you made requests in prayer and then been too impatient to what for a reply? How did you feel when you finally realized your prayers were answered in a way you did not expect?

What ways can you work on having life discussions or conversations so they become two sided opportunities for help and growth?

Today I will…

Chapter 20

Long Division...

FAITH: *"I, then, a prisoner for the Lord, urge you to live in a manner worthy of the call you have received, with all humility and gentleness, with patience, bearing with one another through love, striving to preserve the unity of the spirit through the bond of peace: one body and one Spirit, as you were also called to the one hope of your call; one Lord, one faith, one baptism; one God and Father of all, who is over all and through all and in all."*
~*Ephesians 4:1-6*

REAL LIFE: *"It was pride that changed angels into devils; it is humility that makes men as angels."*
~*St. Augustine*

The practice of mathematical long division is something we have gotten away from. Our children are taught to use calculators at a young age. They do not practice math skills in a manner which sharpens their brain to find an answer without assistance. In another realm, the overall concept of long division is not dead; it's quite alive. Long division was once a positive practice to help us find answers for simple equations in math. However, if we look at what the phrase long division means to relationships, we see the negative impact it has to rob us from being good to one another in our personal and professional lives. To our detriment, the world today seems to thrive on the energy of us not being united, but rather a divided people. This hurt and trial of separation becomes longer and longer. Our responsibility should be to force an end to this separation that has cost us our values, our perspectives and in some cases our communities.

While attending a funeral some time ago, I watched the interactions of the children of the deceased and observed them conversing with each other. In some cases, I overheard what they said to each other, as well as snippets of chats with other family members about their siblings. Then it hit me! At a time when the family should be standing together for comfort, they were actually divided. The focus of the wake centered on differences they had with each other, negative moments they had with their father, and ultimately began to focus on insignificant details like, "Why did that person get to be in charge of that planning detail?" I will admit, I was close to the man who had passed and this was particularly hard for me to witness. My memories of this man were fond and he was an extremely faith filled person. Stunned by what was transpiring, I had to ask myself the question, "Was this the evil one's last effort to destroy a family that was so blessed to walk with a saint?" This question remains unanswered. I do know one thing, without recognizing the long division tearing apart their family; they will certainly never become the unit their father longed for them to be.

Jesus came into this world to unite. Even in His moments of death on the cross He was planning for other people, making sure they would be taken care of so His church would flourish at all costs. His ultimate focus did not take on thoughts of the betrayal He endured, the denial He witnessed nor the loneliness He felt. Jesus' thoughts were to provide for His mother and the disciples He loved as we see depicted in the Gospel of John (19:26-27), *"When Jesus saw his mother and the disciple there whom he loved, he said to his mother, 'Woman, behold, your son.' Then he said to the disciple, 'Behold, your mother.' And from that hour the disciple took her into his home."* Also, His compassion focused on forgiving those who brought our Savior to death: *"Father, forgive them, they know not what they do"* (Luke 23:34). Finally, redeeming the sins of the good thief next to Him with a promise:

"Amen, I say to you, today you will be with me in Paradise" (Luke 23:43). His purpose was to bring people together through an undeniable example of selflessness and continue to find ways to take care of those who still needed to be healed. The plan His Father sent him to fulfill would only be able to prosper if His people came together because of what they witnessed. They would become a community of believers working to spread His word as disciples in the world, bringing harmony to all who believed. Along these same lines, we need to look past our differences, working to be one unit to accomplish all we are meant to be together.

Evil will attempt to destroy anything that brings about love, happiness or hope. If we are able to remain united then we have a greater chance of recognizing where the devil is working to divide us. By working even harder to multiply acts of kindness on every level, we will be rewarded with immeasurable grace which will fulfill us. This favor poured into us from God will be the bonding agent to keep us together, driving evil selfishness from our lives, families, homes, churches and communities.

If we choose to remove the exercise of long division from our calculations to find a sum in math, then let us also remove it from our lives when trying to find the "difference" separating us. Compromise at all costs and give of yourself in ways to assist in bringing all of us together. We do not need to prove we are worthy or that we are able to do things better than another person. Acts of appreciation, which build togetherness, should be done with humility to allow love to conquer all. Faith in each other and trust in the Lord is about looking past long division.

Are there situations or relationships in your own life where you once were bonded but now have become divided? How can you change it?

Who are some people you know in need of prayers to help bring an end to a period of separation?

Today I will…

Chapter 21

We are the Real Celebrities...

FAITH: *"When they had finished breakfast, Jesus said to Simon Peter, 'Simon, son of John, do you love me more than these?' He said to him, 'Yes, Lord, you know that I love you.' He said to him, 'Feed my lambs.' He then said to him a second time, 'Simon, son of John, do you love me?' He said to him, 'Yes, Lord, you know that I love you.' He said to him, 'Tend my sheep.' He said to him the third time, 'Simon, son of John, do you love me?' Peter was distressed that he had said to him a third time, 'Do you love me?' and he said to him, 'Lord, you know everything; you know that I love you.' [Jesus] said to him, 'Feed my sheep.'"* ~John 21:15-17

REAL LIFE: *"Men should be what they seem."*
~William Shakespeare

There is a major disconnect in where we gather our hope and inspiration from these days. As a society, people look to the rich and famous, follow those who have been granted public accreditation or fixate on individuals whose platform is recognized by mainstream media outlets. What happens, more and more, is we get sucked in. We search for answers to our own problems and look for explanations to our struggles within the whirlwind lives of those we glorify as "celebrities." Fact is, w*e are the real celebrities.* We need to relate to our brothers and sisters who are in the trenches with us and not put unrealistic expectations of success on ourselves by comparing who we are to the rich and famous. If we can take hold, realizing that we are the real celebrities, we will put true value on what is important. As the real celebrities, we are writing and re-writing our own scripts each day, in the manner we choose to act out our lives in the world.

While the word "celebrity" means "fame" in the English dictionary, "celebritās" (its Latin origin) means "festal celebration." If we look at it from this angle, we see fame is not at all what we should be seeking; we need to celebrate the good we can offer to each other through stories of victory and failure. It is vital we move beyond the barrier of the fame a mainstream view of celebrities creates. We are all on even playing fields trying to make it through another day. What better way to prove this than a real life screenplay showing us how our role is to find the positive attributes in every person's life? This level of living builds a bond, helping us to believe our hurts and our trials are all solvable. The advice we get and the real life celebrities we focus on, will show stories of triumph, providing light at the end of the tunnel.

When you really think about individuals who offer inspiration, the percentage of people living their normal, everyday lives out in the world, compared to those who are in the spotlight, is immeasurable. It's impossible to run to a TV personality and ask them for advice, nor do we always have access to the evangelizers who inspire us. Those prominent figures we put on a pedestal cannot live up to the expectations we place on them. Most often they somehow end up disappointing us along the way. The hope for us is that we do have family, friends, mentors and co-workers around us who can challenge us to grow just as well.

There is a story highlighting an encounter when Pope John Paul II met a man on the street who was an ex-priest. This man had fallen on hard times, a shell of his former self, ultimately becoming a homeless beggar. With compassion and the heart of a servant, the Pope invited him for dinner. During the course of the evening, after dinner was finished, the Pope asked for the homeless ex-priest to hear the Holy Father's confession. Humbled by the request, the man first refused until the Pope reminded him, "We are all just beggars in this life." Eventually, the man complied with the Pope's request. If we are strong enough to see that each one of us is a struggling beggar, nothing more, nothing less, then we begin to witness how we are in this together. Pope John Paul's example shows us that when it comes down to it; Christ is evident in all of us at all times. Even the head of the church is not above asking the once *broken* beggar for hope and forgiveness through his trials on this Earth.

Do not get caught up in what television and tabloids suck you into believing. No one in this life is more important than the next. Sure, labels are placed and experiences dictate perception, but we are all equal in the end. We are the real celebrities because day in and day out, we fight for our families and we battle for our beliefs. The advice you are able to offer might make you a rock star to that one person who desires a real celebrity to get them through this day. The spotlight is on you to live with a purpose, allowing me to be your servant and for you to be mine, too. Don't miss the chance today to help re-write the ending of someone's story, someone who desperately needs you. Only then, will our "walk of fame" lead us to Heaven; the place where only happy endings exist.

How do you recognize the instances where you have the power to be a true influence to others?

Describe a time when you were humble enough to see someone who had fallen and you helped elevate them to a position where they were an inspiration to you?

Today I will…

Chapter 22

Needing a Victory...

FAITH: *"Put on the armor of God so that you may be able to stand firm against the tactics of the devil. For our struggle is not with flesh and blood but with the principalities, with the powers, with the world rulers of this present darkness, with the evil spirits in the heavens. Therefore, put on the armor of God, that you may be able to resist on the evil day and, having done everything, to hold your ground."* ~Ephesians 6:11-13

REAL LIFE: *"Many of life's failures are people who did not realize how close they were to success when they gave up."* ~Thomas Edison

Ever have those feelings, where once again life gets in the way and reminds us that some days "the world" just wins? I think we all do and look into the abyss of the day and say, "All right, I quit! I have had

enough for today." Then we head off to bed to try again tomorrow. I must say, there is a big difference for those who choose to remain faithful and hopeful despite days like this. It's a conviction in our hearts believing tomorrow, and most days, we will win again and again. We are always in need of victories over adversities in order to help brush ourselves off and put the pieces back together again.

For athletes or dancers, training hard for competition does not mean you will always win. Along the same lines, neither does praying nor offering up yourself to God mean you will never have bad days. Inevitably, the deeper you grow in faith, the harder evil will work to destroy you or pull you further away from God, more than ever before. Think about it, when any team in sports is at the top of the standings, every team wants to beat them. The teams in last place have something to shoot for and can say, "We beat the best." It's their Super Bowl. Satan is no different; he wants to say to God, "Look at how weak I have made your loyal servant and what I have made them do this time. Guess they are not as strong as you thought!" It's at that time God steps in with a never-ending love, coming to our aid. Our Deliverer gives us everything in our life to provide the much needed rebound and victory. He is saying to each of us, *"I got your back and will never let go."*

Satan is a cunning and incredible (albeit nasty) competitor. He knows you so well; all your weaknesses are apparent and he will work to attack them from places you may never expect. In Matthew 4:1-11 we watch the devil dance with Jesus as He is fasting in the desert. The prince of darkness shows Jesus all He can have if He just throws away his commitment to His Father and worships evil instead. It's even more interesting when Satan eventually attempts to use scripture against the One who authored it. Knowing the most Holy Son was vulnerable to this sort of temptation, we must never forget just how susceptible we are to the same type of tactics. It's an illustration reminding us, that we must know who we are called to be. We are equipped with the proper tools to defend a faith that offers us so much. At various points in time, we may think we can relax in our "desert of integrity" consisting of our good deeds, a positive attitude and a willingness to spend time being who we are called to be. The danger within these moments is that we tend to relax because we think we are invincible. On our soap box, the devil stands next to us attempting to poke holes in what we stand for and believe. In those times, it's our duty to remember how Jesus handled the situation and be strong to not throw away our values.

My advice is simple, "When you have a defeat, take the lesson in humility and move on." We are armed with the power of the cross and it is the ultimate weapon in battle. Jesus allowed His captors to defeat Him on Good Friday but He came right back at them with a mighty hand by fulfilling the prophecy on the third day and rising to solidify the church. Even in this, there is a correlation to our humanity and how we handle ourselves. It's vital to see it was not His victory, but a victory for those who believed already; just as much as it was for those who would now be converted, knowing He truly is the Son of God.

Last but not least, be grateful you have an opportunity to fully participate in the game of life. There are so many people who do not have the ability to fight for themselves and others whose time is up, not being afforded another day. Take your pain, take your angst, take your adversity, and offer it back to Him through prayer and service to others. He wants you to win, so define your foe, stand strong in the light of God and go make a new victory when you are in need of one by taking on the armor of God's grace.

What do I consider a victory in life?

What am I equipped with to fight the spiritual battles that may come up?

Today I will...

Chapter 23

You Want Me?...

FAITH: *"For I know well the plans I have in mind for you — oracle of the LORD — plans for your welfare and not for woe, so as to give you a future of hope."* *~Jeremiah 29:11*

REAL LIFE: *"Consult not your fears but your hopes and dreams. Think not about your frustrations, but about your unfulfilled potential. Concern yourself not with what you tried and failed in, but with what is still possible for you to do."* *~Pope John XXIII*

At some point we look in the mirror and assess who we think we are. We have a tendency to take things one step further, assigning names we believe define us: *Success, failure, leader, follower, thin, fat, over-achiever, under-achiever,* etc... With all of these labels, how could we possibly be the ones called to be the difference makers in the world? Our own self image either tells us we are too good to get caught up in a bad situation, or on the flip side, we are not worthy to assist in solving a problem that doesn't concern us directly. This scenario leads us to offer up the question to God, "You want *me?*" before we jump into action. We basically say, "How could I possibly be the one needed to handle a dilemma I didn't create or don't deserve?"

We are faced with an internal conflict anytime we are called to do something we don't want to do. Immediately we think there has to be a mistake and we should not be asked to do such a thing. You have to realize, you are placed in a situation because it's what you are called to be. No one person has it easier than the next, and we all must play our roles. Our only decision is whether we do it willingly with grace or begrudgingly with a sour attitude. One thing is for certain, your actions have an effect. "With great power comes great responsibility" goes the line from *Spiderman,* and each of us possesses more power to help others than we know.

God doesn't make mistakes. Furthermore, He doesn't ask you to do anything He won't help guide you through. We are energized with enthusiasm and talent to conquer negative situations with Him at our side. We are lifted up and made strong to be at the side of those who need us in order to overcome their weakness. Sure, there are situations out in front of you that may seem unfair and goals which appear unattainable, but God needs you to take hold of them. He wants you to prosper so others can be fed by your determination.

After the *Miracle on the Hudson*, the US Airways flight 1549 plane that crash landed into the Hudson River, there was an interview with the pilot on the television program *60 minutes*. Katie Couric asked Capt. Chesley Sullenberger how he landed without destroying the plane in the process. Sully replied, "I believe that everything I have done in my life prepared me for that moment." Within this profound statement, we could change the way we look at so many things in our own lives. Each and every day we are being prepared in the same way for the moment when we are called to respond. So when we look up and say, "You want *me*?" we should quickly add, "Well, you got me." Let God know you understand each day you are being primed to step in to the role you are meant to play at any given time.

The next occasion your moment of resolve is thrust upon you, don't fall back on the negative words you think describe you. Instead, react with belief and consent. God has placed you where He wants you; it's who He wants you to be. Even more importantly, instead of retreating to the labels you once gave yourself, think of all the new titles which can identify you today and always through your action: *Humble, vulnerable, giving, trusting, convicted, problem solver and child of God.*

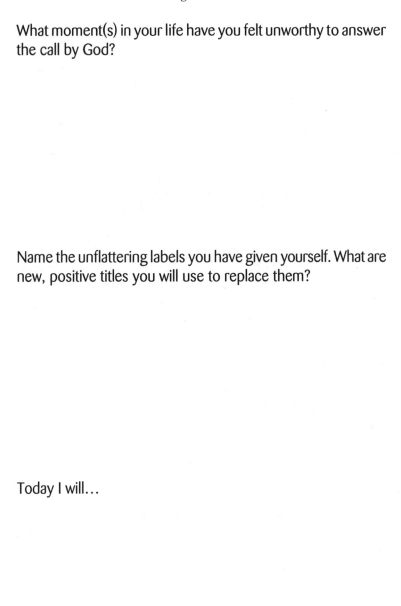

What moment(s) in your life have you felt unworthy to answer the call by God?

Name the unflattering labels you have given yourself. What are new, positive titles you will use to replace them?

Today I will…

Chapter 24

Look for the Surprises…

FAITH: *"Those who love me I also love, and those who seek me find me. With me are riches and honor, wealth that endures, and righteousness." ~Proverbs 8:17-18*

REAL LIFE: *"Reflect upon your blessings, of which every man has plenty, not on your past misfortunes, of which all men have some." ~Charles Dickens*

Family occasions, special events and holidays are so good at bringing out the worst in people. Yes you read that right, they bring out the worst in people. It's a strange twist, a time that should be most centered on family, community, faith and hope, suddenly becomes a period of stress and aggravation. We are so consumed with what we have to do, or what others are doing, we lose the reason we were getting together in the first place. So the advice is simple: "STOP!!" We have to realize, regardless of any circumstance, that those we love will not always be in the same place or always on the same spiritual page as we are. Although it can be frustrating when others don't relate to us, it really is up to us to restore the beauty we cherish in our day.

You have to create the beauty in the moment sometimes instead of waiting for it to hit you in the face. You have to be the one to look for the everyday surprises hidden in each encounter. You have to see the blessing of people in your life for who they are and not for whom you expect them to be. I had to learn the hard way (after many ruined occasions) that no one is going to do these things for me and I'm willing to bet it's the same in your life.

The passage of Mary visiting Elizabeth comes to mind when I think of fantastic reminders of how a surprise can also bring about affirmation for what we struggle to believe. In such a difficult time of being unsure and overwhelmed about her call, Mary went to visit her cousin who was also with child. Both of these pregnancies were miracles, or "impossibilities," for different reasons. Never could Mary have realized the unbreakable connection between the two growing beings inside her and Elizabeth. Yet, in God's presence they both recognized the truth of their call as the encounter is depicted in Luke 1:40-44, *"When Elizabeth heard Mary's greeting, the infant leaped in her womb, and Elizabeth, filled with the holy Spirit, cried out in a loud voice and said, 'Most blessed are you among women, and blessed is the fruit of your womb. And how does this happen to me, that the mother of my Lord should come to me? For at the moment the sound of your greeting reached my ears, the infant in my womb leaped for joy.'"* In this moment, a comfort was brought to both of these holy women as this *surprise* act was one which showed a physical sign of reassurance to what the Angel had told them. A surprise showing real life proof for their faithfulness.

If you have been on a retreat, spent a day alone with just your thoughts or even had the opportunity to pray during that spa day you deserved so badly, then you are fully aware of how the "high" of your experience can end when reality creeps in. So how do we keep our spirit lifted when everyday life wants to take over? It's certainly not easy, but we have to do it or what we believe really wasn't worth the time we took to be reconnected to our faith. I personally strive to look for the everyday surprises that bond me to God, knowing He is still with me even though my prayer period ended. Often times it's through people He has placed along the way to help me discover what I am called to be. Every once in a while we have those life giving conversations where there is an undeniable connection between what we were questioning about life and a cherished companion who is advising. I love when my friends show a genuine interest in my life. Even in just the way a colleague shares my enthusiasm as we talk about ministry and our common love to offer inspirational messages. We must find these kinds of people and let them surround us to be our everyday surprises, showing us the Lord is with us. I long for moments of surprise when my "spiritual high" begins to fade. All these types of reminders have been put there for support and not simply for me to have another friend; wonderful and amazing God incidences of reassurance.

Sometimes we must force ourselves to be grateful despite our need as people, to immediately get caught up in all the inconsequential aspects of life. Don't let it happen, look for the surprises in the day. Trusting and being faithful involves a belief others just may not understand today, but by your example of living it they will be guided in the future. However, you must know you can't do it alone. We must be there for each other. You can't be the light of Christ if you don't allow others to help light the flame for you every once in awhile. We are all just children of God doing our best to rise when we fall with dignity. Our lives are a discovery in seeing what surprises God has in store next.

Who can I offer a surprise to with a phone call or a visit?

List/Name 10 surprises this week that have been blessings.

Today I will…

Chapter 25

We Are Family...

FAITH: *"Faithful friends are a sturdy shelter; whoever finds one finds a treasure. Faithful friends are beyond price, no amount can balance their worth. Faithful friends are life-saving medicine; those who fear God will find them."* ~Sirach 6:14-17

REAL LIFE: *"The language of friendship is not words but meanings."* ~ Henry David Thoreau

As I searched for the right title for this reflection, the lyrics of the Pointer Sister's song *"We Are Family"* immediately entered my mind. In my opinion, it is an overplayed tune at most weddings and family parties where distant relatives show their lack of rhythm, but I digress. Nevertheless, it is very fitting for conveying the deep bond faith can build. The theme of the song actually allowed me to lose myself in a much deeper train of thought and prayer. The following is a journal entry of mine regarding a mass experience which led me to realizations beyond just the readings and prayers that day:

Before mass even started this week, I was invigorated! I got to meet up with some dear family friends in the gathering space as we walked in. We also happened to be joined by two other very close friends of mine. We all decided to sit together which is not a normal occurrence (we are usually all scattered about in various areas of the worship space). Truth be told, most weeks, I am a music ministry 'widower' (no that is not literal, it just means I only get to sit with my wife every week during the homily when she can sneak away from sharing her beautiful talents with the choir); so it is usually just me and the children. But here we were all together and the power of the Spirit was among us. It is almost as if the church becomes brighter and you see everyone just a little different amidst the comfort of family. Then it popped into my head we are family through the faith we share. These are unbreakable bonds shared by people who do not lose a beat even-though time does not play in their favor; we really aren't able to get to enjoy each other's company too often. In looking back at this family we have, I realize we have run the gamut of emotions together. We laugh, we cry, we hug and we share all of the things words are not necessary for. It is a real and true binding friendship.

To extend this overwhelming feeling we are family, it also happened to be the weekend of the "Anointing of the Sick." This is always a very emotional blessing for me to witness because I realize how lucky I am, in so many ways. How fortunate we are in not having to be one of the ailing who stands to receive prayers for healing. Still it happens, the shocking realization occurs to me that we do not always recognize those who are suffering. You see one particular family who seems to have it all together and always have smiles on their faces only to witness in this moment they are hurting more than I could have thought. One of them has come forth; they are battling a severe illness. I have to sit and ask myself, "Who am I to think my problems are the only ones to exist in this world?" Ultimately, real community, real family is evident in the anointing because, we take on the pain of those afflicted with illness. We absorb their trials and then offer them back to God in prayer for comfort and hope amidst their ordeal. I admit I cried through most of the service, not only in the emotion of prayer, but humbled to be blessed in so many ways I do not always stop to give thanks for.

In every sense of the word, we ARE family. All of us are part of something bigger. Our days are lived out in the open for those we care about to see and feel with us. Just as I share with you my thoughts in the hope of inspiring others or providing comfort, I also receive words back to me, healing my hurts. Every time I get a letter or an email which outlines changes others are making out in the world, I am re-energized to go on even when I feel I have nothing left to give. We all have our place in the family tree and you can either be the roots of strength for someone else to rely on or simply be the branches to extend the beauty of this world for all to see.

People who have helped me or can help me in my faith walk are...

True friends offer healing. What can you do to let others know you support them?

Today I will...

Chapter 26

Phantom of the Opera...

<u>**FAITH:**</u> *"For the Lord does not reject forever; Though he brings grief, he takes pity, according to the abundance of his mercy; He does not willingly afflict or bring grief to human beings."* ~Lamentations 3:31-33

<u>***REAL LIFE:***</u> *"They cannot take away our self-respect if we do not give it to them."* ~Mahatma Gandhi

Up in his balcony the Phantom watched the inner workings of the opera productions around him. From afar, he admired a beauty he felt was not within his grasp. Behind a curtain, out of sight and disfigured with scars, it was his own insecurity that caused him ultimately to be shunned. Completely ashamed, he created a persona and a view of who he was. His image would frighten away others with the belief he was a monster. Despite what he thought, he was not completely broken by any of this. Only in appearance, half of him would be considered "not normal" and was covered by the mask which would outwardly exhibit a false sense of dignity. The mystery actually became the character he allowed the world to see, rather than the person he was meant to be.

How many times can we say this very thing for ourselves in our own lives? We are so ashamed by the scars defining us that we do not feel anyone could love us. We try to cover them up, believing there is no way anyone would be willing to look beyond our past and give us a chance to display what we are about. Whether these scars are physical or emotional, our theory does not support a way in which other people could actually get beyond the initial shock after learning some of our deepest issues or past transgressions. What we fail to accept is that each one of us wears a mask because of insecurities and sin; in some cases, to cover the other face we long to hide. It can be detrimental to our relationships when we do this and not allow people to accept all of us. Imagine what it's like with God.

After all, wasn't it the nail marks and lance wound Thomas longed to see in order to make him a believer in the resurrection of Christ? Had Jesus been made completely whole again or worked to hide His scars, there would have been no proof for the doubter. Each hole in His body became a reminder that He was the one who endured the cross for us. John 20:27-29 says that Thomas should not have had to see to believe but should have trusted his faith alone. *"Then he (Jesus) said to Thomas, 'Put your finger here and see my hands, and bring your hand and put it into my side, and do not be unbelieving, but believe.' Thomas answered and said to him, 'My Lord and my God!' Jesus said to him, 'Have you come to believe because you have seen me? Blessed are those who have not seen and have believed.'"* Isn't this how we act in a society where we must see the scars of a person before we can acknowledge their pain? Many times the answer is, "Yes" but it ends with only a superficial recognition of what others truly are. Ultimately, Thomas did not need the scars of Jesus because once he saw Christ in front of him, all was revealed. This level of belief should be the way of finding good in those around us. If we truly look inside another's soul we should not need to hear about their ultimate pain before we recognize them as another wonderful work of creation.

Often times in life, it is our scars and our experience people seek in order to validate us. If someone has been through a struggle or been forced to deal with unique life experiences, it is only through that journey someone is then considered an expert. As a former business executive, I've seen business from all sides. I do not care how much book knowledge a university prepares you for, you can never be fully prepared for the single most unpredictable variable: the human element. Life's lessons shape us and form us in ways we can never set out to predict; sometimes they even develop us into people we do not wish to be. The only way it is possible for all of us to be understood, is to create opportunities of openness where our shortcomings can be lifted up by others and our assets can be infused into the lives of those who need healing. God uses our wounds and our faults to form us as followers if we allow Him. Otherwise, it is the evil around us that has won this battle because it has caused us to become withdrawn; hence we are eaten alive by what we can't control and our own disguise can end up suffocating us.

Take the initiative to find out what hurt people have experienced before you pass judgment, form an opinion of the type of person they are or even cast them aside. It's imperative we find ways to offer a benefit of doubt for people who are distant, wearing masks, watching from afar because they do not wish to reveal their scars to us; should they really have to?

Just as Thomas did with the risen Lord, we must peer into them to know they have endured trials without them offering up their scars as a sign of suffering. I can't always explain why we as people need to see to believe, but there are many people out there who have gone through more than we can imagine, they wear masks to hide all they dislike about themselves. Our focus should be one of faith outreach to not let someone's self image rob them of the beauty on life's stage. We are all members of the cast in the production of life, and we must support one another until the final curtain call.

What scars are you hiding which prevent others from appreciating who you truly are?

Are there others in your community whom you have judged before without knowing their whole background story? Name some people you feel you have wrongly perceived and you need to learn more about.

Today I will…

Chapter 27

Pass the Basket...

FAITH: *"The one who supplies seed to the sower and bread for food will supply and multiply your seed and increase the harvest of your righteousness. You are being enriched in every way for all generosity, which through us produces thanksgiving to God, for the administration of this public service is not only supplying the needs of the holy ones but is also overflowing in many acts of thanksgiving to God." ~2Corinthians 9:10-12*

REAL LIFE: *"From what we get, we can make a living; what we give, however, makes a life." ~Arthur Asche*

Every Sunday at mass we pass the basket while young and old dig in their pockets for a monetary offering to support the church which gives them a place to worship each week. Some people give a little, some give more, while some simply look at it go by without adding anything at all. Each member of the congregation has to decide the best contribution they can offer based on their financial situation. Regardless of our own state of affairs, never for one second do we ever think about taking anything out of the basket as it goes by; after all, it is called an "offertory." So, the question arises, "Shouldn't life be the same way?" Why do we think we are always so entitled to take something out of life rather than putting something in? We must ask ourselves, "What am I putting in to the everyday 'offertory basket' of life?"

Each day, symbolically speaking, we *pass the basket* around in conversations we have with strangers, relationships we hold dear and the roles we play in our colleagues lives. People we interact with need us to contribute to their life in faith, hope and belief. You always have the ability to offer time to listen, care, advise, smile, assist, cry and "be" whatever gifts a person may need for different life giving interactions; the call is to plant the seed.

We all know the story of the fishes and the loaves (John 6:1-15), but the story would never have happened if the people didn't have anything to put in the baskets to start. Jesus doesn't provide the food, the disciples do. Jesus asks them, *"What do YOU have to offer?*" Only after they have put in their offering, Jesus is able to break the bread and provide the miracle of multiplying what His followers put into the baskets. There is another interesting point in this story that can be missed at the end if we do not pay attention. There were leftovers and the people gathered them up so the blessings could be shared with even more people; there were no take home baskets in those days. "*...they collected them, and filled twelve wicker baskets with fragments from the five barley loaves that had been more than they could eat*" (John 6:13). We see the masses didn't just keep taking and taking; they also gave back. The same is true in our own lives. God takes the emotional investments we add to the basket first, and then puts His touches on it so we can feed even more of the multitudes than we originally intended.

While discussing both of our individual speaking ministries, my friend Mike Patin reminded me to ask myself, "What are you going to offer back from the gifts God gave you?" I have carried this reminder, albeit advice, in all my travels as I speak. I even carry it through to my expectations of the overall vision of where my ministry leads me. If I am offering it all up to God, then He will bless it so people longing to be fed hear what is intended for them to hear. Ultimately, I will be nourished by their leftovers.

Our talents, gifts and blessings are just on loan and if we do nothing with them then they are wasted. If we do not share part of us in *the basket* of helping others be whole, than we are just wandering this Earth in a lonely existence of denial never acknowledging where all our blessings come from.

Where can I contribute more with what I have been gifted?

Name some ways you will work to "pay it forward" in order to multiply God's blessings.

Today I will…

Chapter 28

Moving Sidewalks...

FAITH: *"Do not conform yourselves to this age but be transformed by the renewal of your mind, that you may discern what is the will of God, what is good and pleasing and perfect." ~Romans 12:2*

REAL LIFE: *"Coming together is a beginning; keeping together is progress; working together is success." ~Henry Ford*

We see them all the time at airports and at some point we have had to make that decision of what to do on those *moving sidewalks.* Based on our patience level, or time crunch, it is the choice to *stand still, walk* or *run* which can cause us nervous twitches, anxiety and even a search for approval from the travelers in our vicinity. With so many people trying to reach their own destination, there is a lot going on around us. Not everyone is confined to the use of these so called "people movers;" some people are just on the outside going at their own pace under their own free will. In life, we get caught in the same dilemma. As our days continue to move under our feet, we try and decide what might be the best plan to get where we wish to go. I guess you could say, each day is a moving sidewalk in which we are provided assistance with getting to our destination, but it's our decision on how we choose to utilize it. Let's explore the three options of *standing still, walking* or *running* further.

The easiest is *standing still*. After all, we are supposed to just be in the moment and let the moving sidewalk do its work; that's why it's there in the first place. We are still getting to where we need to go and if we have planned accordingly, we can enjoy its intended purpose. However, this could turn into an autopilot situation where we possibly become a little too comfortable. In life, our passive nature could transcend into jarring life decisions which can overwhelm us when we do nothing at all. So even if we are just standing and enjoying, we must be aware that the possibility of a sudden stop is always there.

Another available option for us is to *walk* on the moving sidewalk. In this moment we are proving we want to take initiative. It's an assistance mode where we feel the contraption is aiding us along, allowing us to be helped by the gentle motion of constant movement it provides. We still have the option to stop and pause if we wish because we are not moving so fast. At this pace, we feel the beauty of life around us and we still take time to notice the little things. We are in control, but knowing full well that without the assistance of the mechanism under our feet, we would still be further behind. It's like a prayer that does not overtake our life but moves along with us to reward our faith filled offering.

Lastly, we can *run*. This is a result of poor planning and is certainly not the preferred method in which to make use of the moving sidewalk. We are behind on where we need to be. Our focus becomes more about the goal of where we have to be, rather than the moment we are experiencing. In our day, it means we can miss the smile of a child which provides joy, not recognize the elderly person who needs a helping hand or be attentive enough to hear that phone conversation where we learn the person next to us is lost and needs direction. In the end, we rush to make the destination of our gate. Since God calls us to be shepherds to His sheep, we are required to be attentive at all times. If He notices we are moving at a pace where we have lost sight of what's important on our journey, He may hand us a delay to slow our pace.

This temporary hold-up is a safety mechanism from God for us to have another opportunity to wait and search for all the little things we missed along the way; after all He is a God of second chances.

Use life's moving sidewalk at speeds that benefit your overall purpose and just know it's there to aid in times of victory and struggle; it is supposed to be an assist either way. Think about this analogy: a normal moving sidewalk travels at four feet per second. This means if you walk with its direction, you can go sixty-eight feet in the same amount of time you would walk only eight feet if you were trying to go against the movement of the turn belt. This simply means if you fight what is there to try and help you, you will be further behind than you possibly imagined you would be in the first place. We will still get where we need to be, but only after having to turn around and run that much harder to catch up. Guess the old saying of "go with the flow" has an even greater application than we thought.

Everyone has their own pace and their own decisions to make. Life is not a race and should not be rushed; just because we feel the need to is the wrong reason. Be attentive on your journey knowing, God will never take away time He does not fully intend to give back.

How do I use my time daily to recognize or help the people in my life that need me?

My comfortable pace of life is...

because....

Today I will...

Chapter 29

Too Tired to Fight...

<u>FAITH</u>: *"Come to me, all you who labor and are burdened, and I will give you rest. Take my yoke upon you and learn from me, for I am meek and humble of heart; and you will find rest for your selves. For my yoke is easy, and my burden light." ~Matthew 11:28-30*

<u>REAL LIFE</u>: *"If you are going through hell, keep going."* *~ Sir Winston Churchill*

I will never forget one of the most humbling instances of understanding in what the Lord has asked me to do as an inspirational speaker of faith. While greeting people on their way out of a presentation one evening during Advent, I was approached by a man who was eighty-nine years old. With tears in his eyes, he said, "I want to thank you for allowing me to look at my own situation in a different way than I ever have been able to before in my life." He went on to explain he had his sixty-one year old son with him that night. The son was mentally disabled and had lived with this man his whole life. This man's struggle was that he saw his son as a burden who sometimes robbed him of having his own life. He could not come to grips with his whole life having been about only being a caregiver for his son. What hit him this particular evening was that he realized God calls us into ministry and vocation not just by what we are called to be while in church, but sometimes through the crosses we bear in our own personal life. Where it really caught me off guard was that somehow I'd been able to offer a piece of wisdom or guidance to a man who had most likely forgotten more about living life than I had even yet to experience it myself. We chatted for a while about how amazing I thought he was in caring for his son and how his perseverance, his "Yes," was a courageous example of true love. During this conversation, something else was now happening; my conviction in what I evangelize to our youth about always having a voice, came back full circle to me that night. It was a tremendous honor to know I was able to make a difference through my words to a man who was my elder by many years. How could I look up to the Heavens that night in prayer knowing my struggles at times were nothing compared to the sixty-one years of sacrifice this man had given to his son? Going even deeper, I had to think of all Jesus had given for me, through His long journey on the road to Calvary, to complete His purpose. In life, adversity faces each one of us differently. It seems as we get older, more and more people come to us to be consoled in ways we do not understand. This doesn't even cover the times when we can't find the meaning in our own sufferings. Regardless of whether we are teenagers or in our eighties, the tough times we face are our own to deal with and they affect us deeply. But, when we are "too tired to fight," we need to remind ourselves, and others, there is One above who endured for us; He will never leave us alone in our time of struggle.

I want to share a poem with you which genuinely illustrates that we are neither left alone in our struggles, nor do we have a Savior who is unable to relate to what carrying on at all costs is about. I originally wrote this for my friend's dad, John Schlegel, who was diagnosed with terminal cancer. I now use this prayer for those I know who may need it when nothing on Earth can provide them comfort. It has been sent around the country by participants after talks, I have given it to friends before surgeries and in some cases, emailed it to a person in need who felt they could no longer go on. It's an offering each of us can share when we are unable to find the right things to say that might take away all of someone's fear and angst. These are the words I heard for John that day and have come to realize they are meant for all of us, *always*:

"Too Tired to Fight" ©

When you're too tired to fight...
I am here with a reserve of strength
to pick you up and carry you
when the journey is at its toughest.

When you're too tired to fight...
Relax just long enough
and allow the gentleness of My touch
to softly embrace you and
My presence shall not go unnoticed.

When you're too tired to fight...
I will send My Spirit
to surround you with love
in all those that hold you dear.

When you're too tired to fight...
I shall turn your tears into
"living" water, so that they fall upon your cheeks
with grace and bless the world around you.

When you're too tired to fight...
Remember that I knew you
long before your birth.
Your everyday example is My plan for you.

For it was I who once was too tired to fight...
But that night in the garden
it was **MY** father's hands
that held **ME** as I sobbed.

I was once too tired to fight...
When the road was long, the cross heavy,
the thorns penetrating and
the whip marks throbbing,
but I endured for you.

I was once too tired to fight...
And you were in My heart
as I bowed My head one last time
taking with me all your sin and pain.

Hand in hand we will fight this latest fight...
It is together that all will be revealed
and we shall overcome this battle too,
because I live in you and
My love is never ending.

With Love,
Jesus

Name a recent time in your life when you were "too tired to fight" and why?

How can you recognize the strength of Christ's own struggles and the struggles of others to give us additional grace to bear our own crosses?

Today I will…

Chapter 30

Leave Behind
Your Nets...

<u>**FAITH:**</u> *"You are my shelter; you guard me from distress; with joyful shouts of deliverance you surround me." ~Psalms 32:7*

<u>***REAL LIFE:***</u> *"We're not necessarily doubting that God will do the best for us; we are wondering how painful the best will turn out to be." ~CS Lewis*

So what type of "nets" exactly were the soon to be apostles casting when Jesus called to them? Most likely, we immediately draw the conclusion that these skilled fisherman needed to lay down the tools of their trade to follow Him. Although, I think it goes much deeper and I find a modern day application of our own calling in life.

So many great things are metaphorically taught in scripture, this is one more example. Could it be Jesus was not only talking about the nets they used for fishing? His invitation to them was for complete discipleship, free from all their worldly possessions, including their apprehension. With the thought of walking away from the one thing they knew best to head into something they knew nothing about, there had to be hesitation. They knew the Lord was among them, but what would it really mean to follow Him? Reluctance still had to be within them, despite knowing this call was like no other. If in fact they paused for an instant because they were afraid, we can conclude they were holding on to more than their fishing nets. That's why Jesus was also calling them to leave behind their *safety nets*. No longer would those nets serve a purpose after they surrendered to Jesus' call.

Jesus walked up to them knowing what He would ask of the chosen few and the baggage each one would bring. Recognizing this, we see the significance in His words to, *"Leave behind your nets."* This difficult request made them completely reliant on God. Without the use of their nets and their old ways, Jesus was able to instill in them an open mind to listen and be humbled. Even in our own lives, each of us (in our unique way) has to relinquish something to then go out and follow our intended path in life.

Another aspect in this new way of looking at this particular point in scripture, is delving into how we are able to minister to others. We usually think of using nets as a means to catch fish or as a way to feed the multitudes. However, there are times we need to leave our nets behind in order to use even more of God's tools with open hands. If our hands are always full, then we cannot reach the most amount of people in need. True openness can only occur when we are not stuck within our own comfort zone and we can look to our Creator for complete guidance. No matter how good it is, that old safety net will eventually develop holes in it and will not be able to support us when we need it most. This support has to come from our faith and those God has placed in our lives. After all, if we are dependent upon our safety nets, wasn't there some issue forcing us to use them in the first place? We get lazy and say, "Well, if this doesn't work, then I can always go to the old stand-by."

My own call into ministry came after many years of being an executive who headed up three different companies. Looking back, the Lord had been calling me into ministry much longer than I ever realized. I could see all of the paths He'd been paving and I was walking away from each of them. I was determined not to give up my comforts and safety nets. What I came to realize is, when God has a plan for you, two things occur. One, He will bring you to where you need to be by whatever means necessary. Our denial and holding on to what we think is keeping us afloat just delays the process and forces Him to work that much harder to get our attention. The second thing is that no matter what, we are provided for and His love is a safe harbor nothing can touch. Temporary sadness, fear or apprehension is replaced with an inner peace second to nothing on Earth. I tried just about every crutch and means to secure the level of happiness I longed for. In the end, it's only God's love that brought me to a new level of tranquility through a relationship with Him.

This might be an interesting view for some of us. It's why the Bible places these stories in front of us, in a manner which allows us to apply them to our own life. Each of us needs to think about the time we were called into more, but wanted to hold on to what we knew, even if it was holding us back. Today, I can say nothing amounts to what it is like to drop everything and follow Him. We will catch more fish with our hands if both of them are free from clutching safety nets.

What call have you not listened to because you could be bailed out by something that was safe but is not as fulfilling as your true purpose?

What is one net you need to let go of to fully surrender to Jesus' call in your life? How will it change your life for the better?

Today I will…

Chapter 31
BONUS

The Letters...

FAITH: *"I will lead the blind on a way they do not know; by paths they do not know I will guide them. I will turn darkness into light before them, and make crooked ways straight. These are my promises: I made them, I will not forsake them." ~Isaiah 42:16*

REAL LIFE: *"None of us is as smart as all of us."* *~Japanese Proverb*

As we conclude this portion of our discovery together, it's important for me to write the following letters. These notes are not only something to look at and ponder on, but to reflect on the different type of people we are and responsibilities each of us carry.

To Our Youth,

Never let anyone tell you that you do not have a voice. You should not be viewed as our future but as our hope in the present moment. The world may try to tell you differently, but each of you has a responsibility to be the hands and feet of Christ to those around you. Whether in school or out of school, the times we are most proud of you is for all the things you do positively to represent yourself, your family, the church and our community in the world because it is what is right. (*1Timothy 4:12*)

To Our Adults & Parents,

Our children are dying for us to be hungry in faith *WITH* them. Not only are they fed by those who assist in their journey to know Christ. *You* must give them enough of yourself so you walk with them, leaving the everlasting example and memory of what faith means. This must be carried over into every way you conduct yourself, from family dinners, to family time out, to the sporting events you attend. Be present and most of all, Be God's. (*Ephesians 2:10*)

To Our Elders,

You have seen more in life in your years and relied on God more than anyone. Share your stories of trust and surrender with those who need it. Tell our young people of the importance a relationship with God carries and the real strength which comes with it. Remind other adults what it was like in earlier days when focus can be lost and the consequences suffered in poor choices. Your role is to help prevent life changing mistakes which can lead others away from Christ or, make decisions which harm others. Protect our church with dignity and wisdom. *(Proverbs 16:31)*

To Those Struggling and Those Finding Faith,

God did not intend for us to be alone, not even from the moment Adam was created. You are never more than one prayer away from God or one cry for help from those who long to be your present day Jesus. Take hold of what your purpose is and offer it up in a manner to please the One who made you. Yes, struggle is part of the journey, but never to make you lose hope, rather to make you stronger in choosing to carry on despite what life throws at you. You are part of something bigger than you can imagine. Be a difference maker in this world and I promise you, if you believe, God will never disappoint. *(Isaiah 40:31)*

To Our Church & Worship Community Leaders,

Each one of you has entered into a relationship with the Lord creating a vocational bond only a few can answer. Inspired from each prophets' willingness to proclaim God's message, to Mary's courage to say, "Yes", to the reverent manner each disciple lived out their faith at all costs. You compete for us. We look up to you to guide us as instruments of the Word to walk *WITH* us as we discover God in our midst. Continue to be advocates who minister to us in the same manner Christ did for His church. May you always follow in His footsteps, being a shining light for the world to see. *(1Peter 2:9)*

To Our God,

Thank you for our life giving breath and each way You work to protect us through our days. You are an ever loving Father who forgives every misstep welcoming us into Your arms any time we run to you. We know You are present always to walk with us, love us and embrace each way we glorify Your Kingdom on Earth. It is our goal to please You with our words and deeds and ask You to send your Spirit into our hearts to heal our hurts, provide patience where needed and grant us grace to do Your will with joy. *(Psalms 34:2-4)*

Now it is time to write your own letter to whomever you desire (even yourself as a promise). It can be kept personal or transferred to another sheet of paper...

Dear _____,

Epilogue

Let me begin this closing with the amazing and powerful words of truth spoken by Pope John Paul II while addressing the crowds at World Youth Day in the year 2000 in Rome, Italy. He said:

"It is Jesus in fact that you seek when you dream of happiness; he is waiting for you when nothing else you find satisfies you; he is the beauty to which you are so attracted; it is he who provokes you with that thirst for fullness that will not let you settle for compromise; it is he who urges you to shed the masks of a false life; it is he who reads in your hearts your most genuine choices, the choices that others try to stifle. It is Jesus who stirs in you the desire to do something great with your lives, the will to follow an ideal, the refusal to allow yourselves to be grounded down by mediocrity, the courage to commit yourselves humbly and patiently to improving yourselves and society, making the world more human and more fraternal."

Many people discount God in their life for whatever reasons they see fit. They dismiss His presence in life situations as a coincidence, chalk it up to Karma or wrap the word "philosophical" around it as justification to something other than a divine instance. I am asking you to recognize the "God-instances" happening around you to show you there is truth in the message so many proudly declare.

People are not proclaiming God's word because it is something to rally around for its riches or fame; they are doing it because once you have experienced the realization of His love first-hand in your life, it becomes an undeniable euphoria changing you forever. Making the world a better place happens when we allow faith to influence our real life interactions so when we recognize how they come together, amazing things happen.

I personally see faith being downplayed all the time when people's prayers are answered and they choose not to acknowledge they are of God. It still boggles my mind why people allow denial to control a belief they put so much surrender into only when they are completely broken; although, I spent a lot of my life doing the very same thing. You have this opportunity to say, "Yes, I will recognize, I will look for the wonderful things in the world where His love shines and I will work to make right where hurt exists."

One thing I am sure of is this: If you decide to live a life of faith, you must offer it all to God. There are so many instances where doubt will make you anxious to the point of questioning what you believe. If you are going to let God drive, then let Him drive! I warn you that sometimes you will think He is an awful driver because He is taking you places you do not want to go. In the end, He will take care of you and you will be provided for. The worst place to be on this journey is "in the middle" of sometimes having faith or only running to it when things get so bad you give up. The tendency is to look at faith and prayer as some form of black magic, an instantaneous fix. I have watched others be emotionally drained because they want to believe and yet they cannot commit to falling back on a community that can support them. Those you can rely on wholly in the Lord have the ability to nourish you where you need it most. In the end, this can help you be open to feeding others so they can be fulfilled.

It's my hope that you are now armed with a better understanding of why faith is not something to be viewed as a sign of weakness or a fanatical way of life which blinds your sense of reality. Times will be tough and life will continue but if you allow yourself to take notice where God is present, your life will become about more than you can imagine. Your focus should shy away from the negatives and turn toward the every day events where others need you and you need them. In all of this, you will find God and you will find yourself being nothing more than God created you to be.

TM

About the Author

Greg Wasinski is a full time Inspirational Speaker and Author from Cleveland, OH. Greg's message of faith and real life is delivered in a genuine and attainable way to help people desire a deeper relationship with God while finding the every day application of their faith to encounter the person of Jesus Christ in the world.

As a presenter, he offers family workshops, intergenerational parish missions, men's conference keynotes, staff and volunteer team building sessions and confirmation retreats across the country. Ultimately, it's his passion to meet his audience where they are on their faith journey and provide support to Pastors, parish staff and ministry leaders as they continue to deepen faith formation for their communities.

Prior to answering his call into ministry and founding "Let Me Be..." Ministries, Greg successfully held a career as a corporate executive. He exemplifies a true care for our church's future by opening up dialogue that reminds us why we believe what we believe.

Contact Information:

LMBM Inc.
Greg Wasinski
8584 B East Washington St. #108
Chagrin Falls, OH 44023

e-mail:gw@wasinski.com
www.GregWasinski.com
www.FaithandRealLife.com

"Let Me Be..."
Ministries

all i
ever have
to be...

Reflections:
Greg Wasinski

Vocals:
Aimée Wasinski

"All I Ever Have to Be..." Audio CD is a combination of cover songs featuring the beautiful vocals of Aimee Wasinski, and the authentically genuine reflections of Inspirational Speaker and Author, Greg Wasinski. You'll be sure to find yourself lost in the message to simply be who God created you to be. Perfect to share with family, friends and members of your faith community.

www.FaithandRealLife.com

"Let Me Be..."
Ministries

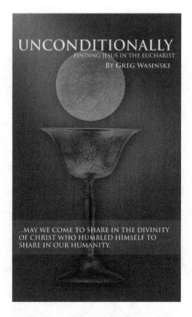

"Unconditionally: Finding Jesus in the Eucharist"
is a book filled with relevant insights, personal reflection,
scripture passages and catechism references illustrating
the ways we are accepted, connected, forgiven, led, loved
and redeemed through the Eucharist. Greg Wasinski
helps readers encounter the person of Jesus Christ in new
ways while surrendering to the grace poured out
through His body, blood, soul and divinity each time we
receive Him at Holy Communion.

www.FaithandRealLife.com